Which Lilith?

Which Lilith?

FEMINIST WRITERS RE-CREATE THE WORLD'S FIRST WOMAN

edited by
ENID DAME, LILLY RIVLIN,
AND HENNY WENKART

introduction by
NAOMI WOLF

JASON ARONSON INC.
Northvale, New Jersey
Jerusalem

This book is set in 11 pt. Garamond by Hightech Data Inc., and printed and bound by Bookmart Press, Inc. of North Bergen, NJ.

Which Lilith? Feminist Writers Re-Create the World's First Woman
was prepared under the auspices of the Jewish Women's Resource Center, a project of National Council of Jewish Women New York Section. This work was submitted in response to a call for prose and poems about Lilith by Jewish women.

Copyright © 1998 by Enid Dame, Lilly Rivlin, and Henny Wenkart.

10 9 8 7 6 5 4 3 2 1

All rights reserved. No part of this book may be used or reproduced in any manner whatsoever without written permission from Jason Aronson Inc. except in the case of brief quotations in reviews for inclusion in a magazine, newspaper, or broadcast.

Library of Congress Cataloging-in-Publication Data

Which Lilith? : an anthology / edited by Enid Dame, Lilly Rivlin,
   Henny Wenkart ; introduction by Naomi Wolf.
      p. cm.
   Includes index.
   ISBN 0-7657-6015-0
   1. Lilith (Semitic mythology)—Literary collections. 2. American literature—Jewish authors. 3. American literature—Women authors.
   I. Dame, Enid. II. Rivlin, Lilly. III. Wenkart, Henny.
   PS508.J4W55 1998
   810.8'0351—dc21   98-9252

Printed in the United States of America. Jason Aronson Inc. offers books and cassettes. For information and catalog write to Jason Aronson Inc., 230 Livingston Street, Northvale, NJ 07647-1726, or visit our website: http://www.aronson.com

Acknowledgments

We gratefully acknowledge the following people without whose help this book would never have become a reality:

Anita Concialdi, who typed our manuscript with care and intelligence and much enthusiasm; Donald Lev, a rare male enabler, who provided constant support and excellent courier service; Zack Rogow, who gave his own time to track contributors; Ruth Sullivan, *Ms.* editor on Lilly's original Lilith piece, for her continuing support and generosity and for her wise editorial advice on this anthology; George Mott, who provided insights into Lacanian thought and for his photographic skills; Barbara Koltuv for her generosity; Terry Noel and Mimi Taufer for their graphic assistance; and a special thanks to Naomi Wolf for her generosity.

Contents

Introduction by *Naomi Wolf*   xi

Editors' Introduction   xv

I OVERVIEW: WHO IS LILITH?

1. Lilith, *Lilly Rivlin*   3
2. Lilith, the Woman Who Would Be a Jew, *Aviva Cantor*   15
3. Lilith at the Red Sea, *Sue D. Burton*   23
4. A Midrash on the Creation of Woman, *Elaine R. Barnartt-Goldstein*   35
5. The Lilith Poems, *Alicia Ostriker*   41
6. Lilith's Version, *Joanne Seltzer*   49
7. Strange Bedfellows: Holy Words and Demonic Images, *Jo Milgrom*   53

II LILITH AND MEN

8. Adam, *Grace Herman* — 61
9. Drifting Like Smoke, *Barbara D. Holender* — 65
10. Lilith, *Enid Dame* — 69
11. Lilith's Version, *Ona Gritz-Gilbert* — 73
12. Male and Female Created He Them, *Nikki Stiller* — 77
13. Adam and Lilith, Adam's Eve, *Henny Wenkart* — 81
14. The First Divorce, *Mary L. Gendler* — 85
15. Lilith's Divorce, *Naomi Gal*, translated by *Suzy Shabetai* — 93
16. Feminist Revaluation of the Mythical Triad of Two Women and One Man: Lilith, Adam, Eve, *Henny Wenkart* — 103
17. The Real First Woman, *Rochelle Natt* — 113
18. Riding the Wind's Wing, *Ruth Feldman* — 117
19. Lilith's Daughters, *Frieda Singer* — 121
20. Divine Mornings, *Susan Gold* — 125
21. Surrounded by Satyrs, Lilith Takes a Stand, *Elaine Frankonis* — 129
22. Lilith Returns, *Elaine Frankonis* — 133
23. Lilith Healing and Aging, *Lilly Rivlin* — 141

III LILITH AS TRANSGRESSIVE WOMAN

24. The First Woman, *Ruth Whitman* — 157
25. For the Lilith Archives, *Mindy Rinkewich* — 161
26. Chameleon, *F. Dianne Harris* — 167
27. Lilith and the Gang, *Sara Eve Baker* — 171

IV LILITH AND OTHER WOMEN

28. The Coming of Lilith (excerpt), *Judith Plaskow* — 179
29. Eden, *Jacqueline Lapidus* — 185
30. Lilith and Eve: Secret Sisters and Successive Wives, *Naomi Goodman* — 189
31. In the Garden, *Susan Gold* — 197
32. Guilt and Knitting, *Elana Klugman* — 201
33. The World of Our Mothers: The Lilith Question, *Frieda Singer* — 205
34. Dancing-Woman, *Helen Papell* — 209
35. Sisters, *Louise Jaffe* — 213
36. Sonnet for a Jewish Woman, *Shoshana T. Daniel* — 217
37. If There Were Angels, *Shoshana T. Daniel* — 221
38. Still Life with Woman and Apple, *Lesléa Newman* — 229
39. Lilith, *Sandy Bodek Falk* — 233
40. A Note about Lilith as Role Model, *Henny Wenkart* — 237

V LILITH AND THE FAMILY

41. Cain and Abel: A Case for Family Therapy? (excerpt), *Alix Pirani* — 243
42. Inside Lilith, *Judith Skillman* — 253
43. The Wellhouse, *Judith Skillman* — 257
44. Kreis, *Judith Skillman* — 261
45. Lilith's Loophole, *Naomi M. Hyman* — 265
46. Postpartum, *Jane Schapiro* — 269
47. Lilith Grows a Garden, *Julia Stein* — 273

48.	Ghazals from a Demon Daughter, *Shoshana T. Daniel*	277
49.	For Lilith: Considerations on Women, Men, Children, and Thinking for Yourself, *Lynn Saul*	281
50.	Cooking a Kid in Its Mother's Milk, *Haviva Ner-David*	285
51.	Lilith and Miriam (an excerpt), *Danielle Storper-Perez* and *Henri Cohen-Solal,* translated by *Ilona Chessid*	295
52.	Sister in the Shadows: Lilith's Role in the Jewish Family Myth, *Enid Dame*	305

VI LILITH AS ARCHETYPE, FEMALE PRINCIPLE

53.	*The Book of Lilith*: A Summary, *Barbara Black Koltuv*	321
54.	woman before the Idea of woman, *Gayle Brandeis*	327
55.	The Story of Lilith and Hawwah, *Savina J. Teubal*	331
56.	Talking about Lilith, *Layle Silbert*	337
57.	Koan: What Is Your Relation to a Flower? *Norma Fain Pratt*	343
58.	Lilith Sighted Starboard, *Susan Gross*	351
59.	Lilith of the Wildwood, of the Fair Places, *Susan Sherman*	355
60.	Lilith's Sabbath Prayer, *Susan Gold*	359
61.	Achsah at the Spring, *Helen Papell*	363

VII LILITH IN EXILE

62.	Lilith, in This Dream, *Leah Schweitzer*	369
63.	Drawn to the Flames, *Nina Judith Katz*	373

64.	Lilith, I Don't Cut My Grass, *Enid Dame*	377
65.	Lilith, Wounded, *F. Dianne Harris*	381
66.	The Last Lilith Poem, *Lynne Savitt*	385

Afterword: Lilith Lives, *Lilly Rivlin*   389
Contributors   395
Credits   405
Index   411

Introduction

Naomi Wolf

Which Lilith? Indeed? Suddenly, emerging within marginal and mainstream culture, there is a multiplicity of faces of Lilith. This subversive, submerged archetype, who has lingered at the very edges of consciousness for so long, is now becoming newly visible. What is happening here?

Jungian psychoanalysis explains archetypes as being the secret, collective, symbolic language that all of us recognize. The fact that Lilith is enjoying something of a renaissance right now—in America at the end of the twentieth century—can tell us a good deal about female needs and longings, once fully repressed, that are surfacing into light. I would say that the emergence of these many faces of Lilith shows that women have reached a kind of critical mass upon their entry into new kinds of power—a critical mass that lets them at last become willing to reacquaint themselves with the shadow side of femininity. It is only when you are truly comfortable with your place in the world—when you have begun truly to possess your identity—that you can look at the less socially acceptable aspects of self, and examine them with more curiosity than fear and aversion.

The resistance, in the past, on women's own part, to becoming acquainted with what Lilith represents has to do with just how profound a challenge she poses. It's well-known that she challenges patriarchy, and patriarchal views of women's "nature" and appropriate status. That explains why she became a sort of closet heroine for some second-wave feminists in the 1970s, who claimed her, in a sense, as their own personal one-woman Act Up guerilla fighter. It was bracing to imagine a figure that could not be subdued or domesticated, a rowdy anti-Eve, a haunting creature who shaped the shadow of female resistance through the ages, whose role was to overturn cozy patriarchal arrangements and let in the chaos made of women's suppressed wildness and fury.

But Lilith, and women themselves, have evolved even further since then—and that is why this anthology could not be more timely. For it is far more challenging, and far more important, to move from the act of reclaiming and re-creating a subversive pro-woman action figure making trouble "out there," to the act of actually integrating her wildness, autonomy, and insurrectionary nature into one's own daily sense of self. Each of the writers in this anthology is, I think, in her own way, doing just that. We no longer need simply a disturbing anti-Eve. We need a positive, powerful, self-directed female archetype to own but also to admire. We've looked around for her. We've tried hard to patch her together out of bits and pieces of character and imagery in films, songs, the clamor of popular culture; we've sought a glimpse of her in the sexual outrageousness of the early Madonna and in the toughness of the early Hillary Rodham and even in the vengefulness of *Thelma and Louise*.

We can't find her qualities reflected in a living woman, and in the movies, well, the Lilith dimension always seems to get its comeuppance. So, not surprisingly, at the end of the 1990s, we turn back in a new way to the original: the legend herself.

What could the archetype offer us, through poems and stories such as these, that we so need right now? First, she offers us a vision of pure female autonomy. Lilith is certainly the opposite of the Angel in the House, the selfless homemaker of the masculine imagination; but she is also far removed from the "good sister" of some kinds of second-wave feminism, the woman who was supposed to submerge her needs and, more profoundly, her individuality, to the good of the collective, or the dictates of the party line. Lilith is the ultimate autonomous woman; and, in a world that attacks as narcissists or as monsters of selfishness women who think too highly of their own individuality or their own needs, it's good to have a figure who can serve us, essentially, as a goddess of the female self; as a reminder that individual character, even to the point of eccentricity, in a woman, is something to honor.

Second, Lilith is devouring. Her appetites are immense. The hunger she manifests is for recognition or reverence, or in the distorted forms her story took in the misogynist Middle Ages, for other people's children or for illicit sexual gratification. However we read her story, she can remind us that it is human, even for women, to hunger. Considering that, if there is a disease of the spirit that could characterize modern women as a whole, it is the terror that one's appetites are excessive and must be controlled, she is a uniquely appropriate reminder for our time that it is only in denying our hungers that they become monstrous.

Finally, she is wise. In the image on the cover of this collection, she is accompanied by familiar representatives of both strength and sagacity: the lions and the owls. Her wisdom was so suspect, as the centuries unfolded, that memory of her sagacity dwindled to stories that she appeared at night in the form of a howling screech owl. Throughout these stories and poems, however, Lilith operates not only, occasionally, as a revealer of wisdom—but also, much more often, as a catalyst for the writer to discern wisdom of her own.

The magic the three editors make in this collection—and the brilliance of Lilly Rivlin in foreseeing what women would need to recover as she founded the excavation of Lilith more than two decades ago—is that through it the reader can do the same. The reader can find her own Lilith—or her own favorite aspects of the many Liliths here who may speak to her. By doing so, she can get at insights of her own that might well remain inaccessible if she were to restrict herself to more ladylike, less Lilith-like, ways of thinking.

Editors' Introduction

In Jewish folklore and rabbinic commentary, Eve was not Adam's first wife. That honor belongs to Lilith, who, according to an eleventh-century Hebrew text, was created as Adam's equal, but who, when he tried to dominate her, uttered God's secret name and resolutely left Eden. Stories about this transgressive female abound in Jewish tradition. Lilith is mentioned in the Talmud, elaborated on in Midrash and in Kabbalah, whispered about in stories, passed down orally, often from mother to daughter. It is Lilith, we are told, who visits men at night, and inhabits their sexual dreams. It is Lilith who is responsible for the unexplained deaths of children. It is Lilith who defies God and the angels he sends, who chooses life alone by the Red Sea over life in Eden with Adam. It is Lilith who sleeps with a variety of human and mythological creatures. It is Lilith, according to Jewish mystical tradition, who marries Samael, the Jewish counterpart of the devil, and who even comforts God in the exilic absence of his feminine counterpart, the *Shekhinah*.

Jewish women have often heard of Lilith, but only in fragments. One learns of her, as Lilly Rivlin says, "dimly, like an archetypal memory." Many of us have been fascinated by her shadowy presence in our culture. We want to know more. What does it mean that our particular tradition, which privileges males in the maintenance of the culture's spiritual life, includes such a powerful female figure? If Eve is "the mother of all living," where does Lilith fit in? Is she, as Naomi Goodman suggests, an older "sister" of Eve's and thus a cultural "aunt"? Does she simply embody male fear of women's power, autonomy, and sexuality? Or is her role more complex? Do women, as well, fear her? Does she represent parts of ourselves we wish to reject? Or is she, in some ways, an empowering figure for contemporary Jewish women? What does she tell us about our culture and its gender expectations? What does she tell us about our possibilities as women and as Jews?

While the figure of Lilith may be as old as Jewish culture itself, her written story takes place in the writings called Midrash—imaginative interpretations or commentaries on Scripture. The author of the eleventh-century text, *The Alphabet of Ben Sira*, in which her story is first told at length, obviously wanted to reconcile the discrepancy between the two accounts of creation in Genesis (1:27 and 2:22). His narrative of an independent, disobedient first wife (which itself probably drew upon older oral tales of such a figure) has become part of Jewish culture, inspiring and influencing other Lilith stories. Until recently, these stories were primarily told by men, and their depiction of Lilith was consistent: she was a witch; a temptress; a dangerous, evil woman.

Modern Jewish women have been turning to Midrash as an attractive and useful way of understanding our own tradition, of locating ourselves within it, and, frequently, of revising and extending it. The roles of Eve, Sarah, Ruth, and Vashti, for example, have been vigorously re-imagined by contemporary Jewish women writers; work by theologian Judith Plaskow, scholar Savina Teubal, poet-critic Alicia Ostriker, and writer Mary Gendler, among others, has formed the foundation for a movement of feminist biblical revisionism. It is hardly surprising that Lilith, although barely mentioned in Scripture (she only appears briefly as a night owl in Isaiah and in the Dead Sea Scrolls as demons—plural—in the Song of Sage), would become the subject of Midrash-making, by these writers and many others. Indeed, there has been an outpouring of work about Lilith by contemporary Jewish women. In re-interpreting the stories of this paradoxically notorious yet little-known figure, Jewish women writers working in a variety of genres are extending the boundaries of Jewish culture and re-defining our place in it.

Editors' Introduction

In this anthology, we offer a vivid, provocative, and enlightening sampling of Jewish women's written responses to the Lilith myth. While some of the women presented here are scholars, this is not intended to be a scholarly work. Rather, it is a collection of contemporary midrash on a subject which—quite definitely—holds great interest and meaning for Jewish women as well as non-Jewish. In Lilly Rivlin's afterword, "Lilith Lives," there is a guide to contemporary "sightings" of Lilith. For a period of eight hundred years, Jewish men known as sages or Rabbis interpreted the Bible, and they called it midrash. Women did not participate in this sacred activity. According to Naomi M. Hyman, in her excellent book *Biblical Women in the Midrash—A Sourcebook*, "Midrash is a way of integrating change and tradition. . . . [It] in not only a means of extracting meaning from the Bible. It is also a way of reading meaning into the text," she adds, explaining the authority of midrash. Hyman correctly notes that "the Rabbis believed that making midrash was a sacred activity." We, the editors, believe that in putting together this anthology, we are providing the space for contemporary women to link themselves to a tradition and participate in a sacred activity. We are infusing energy into Lilith and creating a new tradition.

We define Midrash as a dynamic, elastic concept which may encompass many specific literary genres: the essay, the tale, the short story, the meditation, the poem.

Therefore, we do not find it useful to present this material in genre-determined groupings: all the "fiction" in one section, the "meditations" in another, etc. As the Lilith figure herself eludes conventional categorization, we are not surprised that the writers in this collection make use of a multiplicity of genres to respond to her. Our primary focus, however, is not on genre, but on a very different issue.

In selecting the material for this anthology, we were struck by the regularity with which certain themes—or "stories"—recurred in the works of different writers. Evidently, the writers were using the Lilith myth as a way of talking about our own relationships with men, women, family members in general, and mothers and daughters in particular. Further, this figure enabled us to examine, deconstruct, and often re-envision the concepts of female independence, loneliness, and alienation; and their opposites, commitment and membership in family and community. It is the dialogues that we saw taking place among, as well as within, these writings that we wished to emphasize in this book. This concern determined our organizational strategy.

The writings are grouped in seven parts. The first, an overview of the Lilith story and what it might imply for a modern woman, begins with Lilly Rivlin's classic 1972 *Ms.* article—a work that sparked the subsequent interest in and recovery of Lilith as an important female archetype. Here too we see Susan Sherman's early poem identifying Lilith as an outlaw figure, written out of the official texts, and Alicia Ostriker's recent, playful "Lilith Poems," which bring race as well as gender into this discussion.

Part II, "Lilith and Men," contains, significantly, the largest number of writings. Here we see Lilith in relation to a variety of men and male principles, from Adam to the Jewish God (a situation described in Kabbalah), to Greek mythological characters to more mundane human males. Part III, a brief section, reminds us of the familiar depiction of Lilith as a transgressive woman, though from a woman writer's viewpoint. Ruth Whitman sympathizes with the victimized seductress of her poem, while Sara Eve Baker appears to admire the Satanic punk-leader she evokes.

Part IV examines Lilith in relation to other women, starting with Eve (who is variously friend, co-conspirator, and lover) and going on to include Athena; I. B. Singer's sister, Hinde-Esther Singer-Kreitman; the seductive subject of a painting; and the writer herself. Part V presents Lilith as a way of talking about family relationships, particularly those between mothers and daughters. Here we see Lilith as a symbol of alienation of children from their parents, as a primary figure in a therapeutic case study by Alix Pirani, or as in Jane Schapiro's stunning poem, the embodiment of the violence mothers are capable of feeling toward their children. Paradoxically, however, a number of writings imagine Lilith as a "good mother," granting her children special knowledge or freedom.

In Part VI Lilith appears as an archetype, a creative female force, a symbol of women's generative power. In Savina Teubal's "The Story of Lilith and Hawwah," the Genesis story is re-imagined, with Lilith as the predominant creative force. In Layle Silbert's story, she is both a dim memory of a lost love and an incarnation of Gaia, the earth. Norma Fain Pratt's Zen practitioner envisions her during a retreat at a Buddhist monastery. And Helen Papell, in "Achsah at the Spring," sees her as a powerful emblem of peace in a war-torn, embattled world.

The seventh part includes work in which Lilith appears as a woman exiled (usually by choice) from a partner, family, or human community. The angry speaker in Leah Schweitzer's poem, for example, cannot "seem to find a place" for herself even in her own dream. Nina Judith Katz's protagonist is the eternal outcast, the woman or Jew hunted and killed by powerful, threatened men. In two of the poems in this section, Lilith is an aging woman. In Lynne Savitt's "Last Lilith Poem" she is a suicide who remains, in a sense, alive.

One more point must be made: we have intentionally chosen to focus on Jewish women's responses to the Lilith figure here, not because male or non-Jewish writers cannot do, or have not done magnificent work on Lilith. (Indeed, many of their writings have inspired our own.) Our emphasis, however, is as much on modern Jewish women's search to define ourselves as it is on Lilith. As Jewish women, we are particularly aware of the fact that this myth—the story of this fiercely independent, sexual, undomesticated woman—arose in a Jewish cultural context. Therefore, we must infer that the Jewish culture, for all its privileging of men in the public and institutional sphere and relegation of women to the private and familial sphere, has a need to imagine such a woman—in short, has a need for Lilith. We Jewish women have, in some ways, been shaped by this need. In our writings, however, we are reshaping the story to serve our own needs. It is just this process of Jewish women entering and revising our own tradition that fueled this anthology. However, we encourage and welcome other presentations of Lilith material. We see this anthology as one step in a process of necessary biblical revisionism. We hope it will inspire others.

I
OVERVIEW: WHO IS LILITH?

In some mythology Lilith, not Eve, was the first woman, created simultaneously with Adam. Who is she?

1
Lilith

Lilly Rivlin

Lilith "bound in chains," the inscription on the inside of the body lines, on the outside of the body lines is the priestly blessing. In the body section is written "a protection for the child that he not be harmed," followed by the names of the angels associated with Lilith, Sanoi, Sansanoi, and Samengalof. (From the Feuchtwanger Collection—19th Century.)

In the beginning "*male and female created He them.*" God formed Lilith, the first woman, just as he had formed Adam, from pure dust. Adam and Lilith never found peace together because Lilith contested Adam's claim to be supreme. They were created simultaneously from the same dust, she reasoned, and were therefore equal. When he asserted he was to be her master, she insisted there was no justification for his supremacy. When he wished to lie with her, she took offense at having to lie beneath him. Adam tried to force her obedience. Rather than accept subjugation, Lilith chose to leave Adam and live alone by the Red Sea. She found peace there on the hard-rock-sand lining the deep blue Gulf of Aqaba, making love with satyrs, minotaurs, and centaurs.

I first became aware of the cosmic sexist conspiracy when I realized that nothing of my personal sense of woman derived from any historic female hero—mythic or real. I knew about Lilith, dimly, like an archetypal memory, as a predecessor to Eve. And I was repelled by Eve, that submissive blonde creature wiled by a snake, falling for a line. My own instinct told me Eve should have—could have—walked to the Tree of Knowledge of her own free will, picked the fruit, felt its texture, and—weighing the consequences—eaten if she so desired.

Most of all, I felt deceived by the myth of Eve. It seemed to me that the reaching out for knowledge in the form of the symbolic fruit was both a sensual and a courageous act, an adventure of the spirit and a desire for experience, which the story of Genesis somehow had turned into a debasing act of shame and guilt.

I felt uncomfortable in the Eve role. I twisted at the bit; I felt Dionysian impulses. My personal images were not of an infantile paradise, a protected garden of Eden, but of rough yellow and brown deserts, of iron-gray molten rock, of golden thistles and thorned brambles. Also, I could not understand the shame of nakedness. I was animal, I was God: I was substance and pulsing orifice. Beneath layers of civilization, I was fur throbbing, and echoes of deep-welled animal cries. If I was not Eve's daughter, whose daughter was I?

In setting out to discover Lilith, the first Woman, I followed in the footsteps of all mythic heroes. The first step was to assimilate my opposite; in this case, Eve. For in the journey backward through time, I hoped to arrive at self.

The earliest extant European cosmogony of Lilith (though by no means the earliest of all) is in the *Alphabet of Ben Sira*, an early Jewish commentary on the Bible compiled in the eleventh century. We know that the author drew upon very early Hebrew legends elaborating on the discrepancy that exists between the two Genesis versions of creation (a discrepancy that allows Lilith to be presumed as Adam's first wife). In Genesis II, Eve is an afterthought, an appendage of man. In Genesis I, male and female are created simultaneously. The discrepancy itself is easily explained. Divergence between the two Genesis versions results from a careless weaving together of an early pre-Exile version and a post-Exile Babylonian account of creation.

Genesis, which was far more influenced by earlier polytheistic and matriarchal cults than most pious Jews and Christians would like to admit, was edited from the sixth century B.C.E. onward for moralistic reasons. Zealous Jewish priest-editors tried to expurgate all vestiges of the Canaanite goddess cults that the Israelites themselves had assimilated. The remnant, "male and female created he them" (Genesis I), slipped by those editors. The later legend of the rib is clearly what Joseph Campbell (the contemporary scholar of ancient myth) refers to as a patriarchal inversion (giving precedence to the male) of earlier myths of the hero born from the goddess Earth.

Rabbinical tradition developed the Genesis I version of creation to indicate that God made Adam and Lilith from dust at the same time—some say as twins joined back to back. As there is no philological explanation why the female is called Lilith, we can only conclude that the name was associated with an atavistic female spirit that had to be assimilated or dealt with in some way.

Still, if Adam and Lilith were created at the same time, they were ipso facto equal and this was too subversive a concept to leave unqualified. The author of the *Alphabet of Ben Sira* compiled the "official" myth of Lilith, a story designed to quell any hope for equality:

> God then formed Lilith, the first woman, just as He had formed Adam, except that He used filth and sediment instead of pure dust. From Adam's union with this demoness sprang innumerable demons that still plague mankind.... Adam and Lilith never found peace together; for when he wished to lie with her, she took offense at the recumbent posture he demanded. "Why must I lie beneath you?" she asked. "I was also made from dust, and am therefore your equal." Because Adam tried to compel her obedience by force, Lilith, in a rage, uttered the magic name of God, rose into the air and left him. [*Alphabet*, as quoted in *The Book of Genesis*, by Robert Graves and Raphael Patai.]

She finds peace along the Red Sea. But this idyll is rudely interrupted. Adam appeals to God, and He sends forth three angels to persuade Lilith to return. (Why God and Adam team up is another matter for speculation. Either God was used to support earthly masculine fears, or both God and Adam were threatened by Lilith's sexual demands and independence.) Lilith prefers life without a mate—at least a mate like Adam—to giving up her integrity and independence. Besides, she has tasted the sensual free life beside the Red Sea. The angels threaten her with death for her refusal, but, as the *Alphabet* tells the story, she has a logical response:

"How can I die when God has ordered me to take charge of all newborn children: boys up to the eighth day of life ... girls up to the twentieth day. Nonetheless, if ever I see your three names or likenesses displayed in an amulet above a newborn child, I promise to spare it." To this they agreed; but God punished Lilith by making one hundred of her demon children perish daily.

By taking fragments of earlier myths and placing them within a Jewish framework, the author of the *Alphabet* has transformed a creation myth of male-female equality into a morality play, and the independent woman into a jealous avenger. Lilith may be independent and strong-willed, but she is punished for this sin: Is the severity of her punishment connected to Lilith's sexual openness? The Adam and Eve myth clearly avoids sex. In fact, having eaten the fruit of knowledge, the protagonists, for the first time cognizant of nakedness and sex, quickly make for the leaves.

Lilith, on the other hand, seems to have had no compunction. On the contrary, she is unself-conscious and quite active. Can Adam not cope with her activity? Should we assume he is asexual or undersexed? No, it is that he cannot cope with equality. It might appear unreasonable that sexual independence would call for such punishment, but the entire patriarchal system, which inverted an earlier supremacy of woman, would be threatened by such a declaration of equality.

In one blow then, Lilith is transformed from a co-progenitor into a mother-creator-destroyer, similar in some respects to a sister mythic figure, the Indian Mother Kali, who is depicted simultaneously as an awesome force of life and death. Two right hands of the many-armed Kali hold the sword and scissors of physical death, and her two left hands hold a bowl filled with food and the lotus of generation. But whereas Kali remains a harmonizer of opposites, the divisive Western mind reduces Lilith to her negative and destructive attributes. Lilith is not allowed the depth and multiple reality that Kali's ever-moving hands symbolize. She becomes her opposite: a one-dimensional personification of the destructive life force.

It is not accidental that this myth of Lilith gained popularity among Christians and Jews during the Middle Ages (the time of the height of witchcraft and the cult of the Virgin Mary). Both cultures were threatened by the disintegration of the feudal structure, and in both religions, the orthodox authorities were fighting against liberalizing tendencies. The establishments were involved in esoteric disputations, while the helpless masses sought comfort in superstition.

In medieval Europe (especially in Germany), Lilith became a popular man-devouring creature, a threat to Christian and Jewish homes. She is the envious estranged wife and mother who covets other women's children, and threatens to steal them, unless prevented by charms. In those dark days of man, Lilith also underwent a physical change. Instead of the great beauty of her earlier incarnations (one oriental version depicts her overpowering physical and intellectual gifts), she becomes in the Middle Ages a scraggy-toothed hag. Apparently even Lilith could not withstand the ravages of time. Though ugly and malformed she still prevails, however, as the seductress of sleeping men.

According to the sources of kabbalism, a thirteenth-century mystical movement, Lilith had a very important position indeed. In the *Zohar*, the "bible" of kabbalists, Lilith is the harlot, the wicked, the false, or the black. Here Lilith reaches the pinnacle of evil and becomes Queen of the Underworld. As the permanent partner of Satan, known here as Samael, Lilith is the quintessence of darkness. In that world, she fulfills a function parallel to that of the *Shekhinah*, the Divine Presence, in the world of sanctity. Just as the *Shekhinah* is the mother of the House of Israel, so Lilith is the mother of the unholy fold called the "mixed multitudes." Her ultimate vilification is man's vindication.

Ironically, the very same source—the *Zohar*—also credits Lilith with her greatest hour: she becomes the mistress of God. This unholy alliance is the outcome of the destruction of the Temple and the Exile of Israel. Israel's mother, the wife of God, had to leave her husband to go into exile with their children. As a result of his broken marriage, God consorts with the Other, "the slavewoman Lilith." Only the coming of the Messiah will put an end to God's degrading coupling with Lilith, and will bring an end to Lilith's existence.

The notoriety of the Lilith myth was accompanied by the wholehearted acceptance and use by medieval women of amulets to ward off Lilith. Scribes were designing amulets that evoked the names of the three angels sent to bring Lilith back to Adam. The angels circling the bulbous symbol of Lilith guaranteed the safety of the newborn infant. If the amulet was defective, a circle drawn about the parturient female assured an absolute defense against the evil strangler of babes. These amulets have a long history. A prototype medieval amulet used to ward off Lilith is found on a Persian clay bowl. (Apparently Lilith was no respecter of cultural boundaries.) The incantation on the bowl, which dates back to about 600 C.E., is enough to shackle all the demonic broods in existence: "Bound is the bewitching Lilith with a peg of iron in her nose; bound is the bewitching Lilith with pincers of iron in her mouth; bound is the bewitching Lilith with fetters of iron on her hands; bound is the bewitching Lilith with socks of stone on her feet...." (Amulets still exist today. A few years ago, a Moroccan woman concerned about my barren state presented me with one. Ironically, Lilith had become for her a fertility symbol.)

Clearly, the myth served as a carrier of social values, as a boundary for straying females, and as a convenient totem for men and women frightened by their inner desires. Lilith, in her many guises, was a scapegoat for instinctual (and thus evil) drives. Males could attribute their natural nocturnal emissions to Lilith. How else could they justify this "sinful" flow? Women, half-souls by the going standards, living in a world of supernatural spirits and religious dogmas, could find solace in venting their prosaic frustrations on this symbol of distorted womanhood. It is a commentary on woman's self-hatred that she so readily embraced this deformed and evil archetype.

If infant mortality caused not only personal despair but social stigma, what better way to avoid responsibility than to shift the onus onto Lilith? Ineffectual males, frightened by their own fantasies of the seductive and nightmarish, drew upon the myth and encouraged appendage-complexed Eves to weave charms and carry amulets for protection against their repressed instincts. Lilith's omnipresence, it was believed, could even threaten a man who wished to engage in lawful sexual intercourse with his wife. "Lilith is always present in the bed linen of man and wife when they copulate, in order to take hold of the sparks of the drops of semen which are lost . . . and she creates out of them demons" (Raphael Patai, *The Hebrew Goddess*).

Most damaging, the myth of Lilith prevented community among women. Vital female qualities—sensuality, passion, independence—were associated with a feared, hated, and perhaps secretly envied, female symbol. If any sister-woman exhibited such attributes, she was to be regarded with suspicion. Unable to exalt their mutual qualities and claim kinship, women remained isolated—shackled in the magic circle.

But no amount of distortion by patriarchal rewritings can suppress the ambivalence buried in the symbol of Lilith. In fact, some scholars suggest that the extant myths may have been rewritten from an earlier gynocratic mythology. Is it not possible that Lilith's intention of visiting babies is not to harm them but to sustain them? This other Lilith could have been attending mothers in labor to give comfort, to share pain, to present passion to the newborn child and to welcome life. There were all these possibilities. Perhaps some women sensed them, as I did.

Unsatisfied by the negative personification of Lilith found in the Middle Ages, I resolved to go further back and look closer at the fragments compiled in the *Alphabet of Ben Sira*, to search for a primal form of Lilith that would satisfy that self which had rejected the restrictive myth of Eve.

I encountered Lilith in many guises, taking on many forms, but clearly occupying a central position in Jewish demonology. The lady definitely got around. Some writings identify the two harlots who appeared in judgment before Solomon as Lilith and a sister demoness, Naamah. Widespread, too, is the identification of Lilith with the Queen of Sheba. This notion, which dates back to a third-century source, is based on a Jewish and Arab myth that the Queen of Sheba was actually a jinn, half-human and half-demon. As proof of Lilith's masquerade, it is maintained that the riddles that the Queen of Sheba posed to Solomon are a repetition of the words of seduction that the first Lilith spoke to Adam.

It appears that the male mind, in order to cope with sharp-witted females, could only imagine a demonic explanation: since the Queen of Sheba was very clever, she must have been Lilith reincarnated. The assumption: a clever woman is unnatural; therefore all intelligent women must be allied with demonic powers. But what about the women who took pride in their intellect or were excited by thought? Such women were possibly the forerunners of the Faustian pact with Mephistopheles. Others might have ridden the crest to become shamans, witches, and spell fixers—all common outlets for female intelligence.

In a further transformation of the third century, Lilith becomes a female demon who is known by many names and moves about the world at night, visiting women in childbirth and trying to strangle their newborn babies. The talmudic tradition confused this spirit's name with the Hebrew word for night (*laylah*) and turned Lilith into a night demon, a succubus who attacked men sleeping alone. The offspring of Lilith's nocturnal rapes were the demons that plague the world. Here we have two very separate ancient themes: a seductress who attacks sleeping men and a Mother Goddess with destructive powers, combined for the first time in the moral myth of the *Alphabet*.

Lilith's conversion into a Hebrew demoness probably occurred in the early part of the first millennium B.C.E. It was at this time that the Hebrews invaded and conquered Canaan. Undoubtedly they were influenced by the Canaanites' indigenous goddess worship and matriarchal view of creation. We know, for example, from Deuteronomy that the priests of ancient Israel could not dissuade their females from praying to the Canaanite fertility goddess, Anath. Time after time the prophets denounced Israelite women for following Canaanite practices such as prenuptial promiscuity.

Thus, in establishing their genealogy in Genesis, the Hebrews had to deal with these assimilated beliefs. Joseph Campbell explains the changes this way: the Hebrew patriarchy of the first millennium adapted the mythology of the lands they occupied only to invert it so that a symbol of a myth became the opposite of its origin. "Yet," says Campbell, "there remains an ambivalence in the basic symbols of the Bible that no amount of stress in patriarchal interpretation can suppress."

Classicist Robert Graves and anthropologist Raphael Patai note that "it is characteristic of civilizations where women are treated as chattel that they must adopt the recumbent posture during intercourse." Lilith's refusal to lie beneath became the central issue in the revised Lilith myth. It was obviously a glaring challenge to the accepted sexual mores of the Hebrews. This "unnatural" position, passed from oral tradition to recorded legends, was a stick in the craw of the ancient patriarchs. It had to be suppressed. What better way to put Lilith in her place and to squelch her strange and threatening sexuality than to inscribe her in the nation's codex as an evil and unnatural spirit? For the only appearance of Lilith in the Bible is among the beasts of prey and the spirits that will lay waste the land on the day of vengeance (Isaiah 34:14).

Earlier narratives of Creation sought to embody the relationship between man and woman as a mirror of nature; that is, the universe created by a union of Father Sky and Mother Earth. The monotheistic editor of Genesis could assign no part in Creation to anyone but the transcendental God. This meant a radical removal of the ancient matriarchal deities and a total repression of the surrounding goddess cults. The goddess and priestess had no place in the Hebrew religion. Female worship had to go underground or within the psyche. Lilith lived on under monotheism as the repository for all suppressed matriarchal yearnings.

Lilith lived on within me, and when she disappeared from the Hebrew landscape, I tracked her to still earlier sources. Whence, for example, the name Lilith? In Babylonian and Sumerian demonology of the third millennium B.C.E., "Ardat Lilith" appears as a "maid of desolation," one of several "harmful spirits" occupying mythological space. She is a demon of waste places who preys on males.

In the Sumerian epic *Gilgamesh and the Huluppu Tree* (ca. 2000 B.C.E.), Lilith lives in a primeval willow tree on the banks of the Euphrates. At the base of the tree is a dragon; in his crown live a Zu-bird and its young. Gilgamesh, the hero, slays the dragon; whereupon the Zu-bird escapes with its young to the mountain, and Lilith, terror-stricken, flees to the desert. And is that the end of the journey? Can I rest in the desert?

I trace her back even further to the Assyrian belief that Lilith is a wind spirit, wild-haired and winged. I cling to this image of a lithe female aspect of nature, sometimes calm, sometimes tumultuously sweeping all in her path, lingering over blooming cacti, pressing through shifting sand.

In following Lilith backward through time, I had sought a female archetype that is creative and self-liberating. I found the wind. My journey ended at the beginning—only the wind, moving upon the void (containing nothing and everything within it). And I harness the wind spirit in time and I write a new Creation.

In the Beginning

When God set out to create Heaven and Earth, He found nothing but Tohu Va'Vohu, namely Chaos and Emptiness. Faced by the Deep, God's spirit wavered. In that atomic second, He became aware of Another. It was the pulse of the Universe: a Throbbing Spirit whirling in the Chaos. In that space I and Thou encountered. During that Absence, Energy was born. And He wanted to replicate that second, that memory of creation which He called Order. The Throbbing Spirit called it Love. And the Throbbing Spirit directed Love toward the Chaos, and the Heavens and the Seas divided. And God gave Order to the Energy, and there was Light. And the Throbbing Spirit danced in a golden light until there was Fire. God watched the Fire glow within the Seas and dreamed Jewels. And God and the Throbbing Spirit embraced in Dream and Reality, and there was Spirit and Matter. And God pulled the Light from the bowels of the Fire, and there was Day and Night. Throbbing Spirit loved with such force that the Skies trembled and the Seas boiled, and there was Lightning. The Heavens wept with joy, and there was rapture in the universe.

Throbbing Spirit and God combined Love and Order. She created the Grass, Herbs, and Trees to reciprocate to the Sun, Moon, and Stars. And on growing globules of Energy, He placed Land-beasts and Creeping Things, while the Throbbing Spirit pulsed and kept time. The Throbbing Spirit changed Her rhythm as She encountered the growing globules of Energy, gaining momentum and movement. And the Wind moved among the Heavens and the Seas, along globular islands of Energies sowing grass, herbs, and trees, stroking land-beasts and creeping things with life. And Earth revolved in the Deep.

God sought the Throbbing Spirit in the Wind to ask Her: "What final Order?" "An image of you," She replied. And so God took some of every Element He had created and made Adam. But He took nothing from the Wind. And Adam who was but an image of God existed. And the Throbbing Spirit of Chaos and Emptiness had also faced the Deep and created. She took the Elements and made an image. And She breathed life into Lilith. But the Wind had not passed through Adam, and He could not remember the birth of Love which gave forth Energy. You know the rest of the myth. Adam now knows the myth. He has felt the Throbbing Spirit in the Wind.

2
Lilith, the Woman Who Would Be a Jew

Aviva Cantor

While the women in the Scriptures are somewhat discredited in the Midrash and Agadah, they never actually become negative role models for Jewish women. Even Eve is pictured in the Midrash as a "light-headed," irresponsible, and easily manipulated female (as contrasted with the Christian view of her as evil incarnate).

The prime negative female role model in Jewish mythology is Lilith, who is the flip side of Esther, the altruistic-assertive enabler. Esther is the epitome of enabler, Lilith of *dis*abler.

The story of Lilith draws on various *midrashim* that attempted to resolve the contradiction between the two stories in Genesis about the creation of the first woman. One was that God created her from the earth together with Adam, the other that God fashioned her from Adam's rib. Midrash writers speculated that there were two Eves, and that the "First Eve" was the one created from the earth. Meanwhile, in the Talmud, Lilith is mentioned several times as a wild-

---

* Aviva Cantor's essay originally appeared in *Lilith*, vol. 1, no. 1, 1976, in an earlier version, entitled "The Lilith Question." She has revised it for her recent book, *Jewish Women/Jewish Men: The Legacy of Patriarchy in Jewish Life* (HarperSan Francisco, 1996), from which this essay is reprinted.

haired winged creature with nymphomaniac tendencies and as the mother of demons.

The author of the *Alphabet of Ben Sira*, which scholars believe was written sometime between 600 and 1000 C.E., merged the two traditions, giving us the demon Lilith as Eve's predecessor. The *Alphabet* relates how after God created both Adam and Lilith from the earth, they immediately quarreled because she refused to lie beneath him. Lilith told Adam: "We are both equal because we both come from the earth." Realizing that it was as futile to use logic to argue with him as it was with anti-Semites, Lilith uttered God's secret Name and flew away from Eden. The *Alphabet* tells of her refusal to return to Adam after three angels God had dispatched asked her to. She accepted the punishment that one hundred of her "demon children" would die every day.

Early kabbalistic works, starting with the thirteenth-century *Zohar*, embellished Lilith's demon reputation with sundry legends, often contradictory, of her vengeful activities to harm or kill: newborn babies; women who give birth and nurse in rooms without industrial-strength amulets to ward her off; and men, whom she robs of sperm in their sleep to manufacture demon children or whom she seduces and afflicts with illness. In later kabbalistic works, she is portrayed as the bride and partner of Samael, the archdemon and chief evil force in the universe, who is blocking national redemption. These stories became part of Jewish folk culture, and anti-Lilith amulets are still enjoying brisk sales in some Orthodox communities.

To understand the motivations behind the Lilith myth, we must separate the *Alphabet* story, which is an almost entirely gynophilic one, from the kabbalistic legends, which are totally misogynist. In the *Alphabet*, Lilith is an independent, courageous woman and a strong character. Her self-esteem is high: she perceives her equality with Adam as part of the natural order of things, a result of their having been created from the same element. She immediately recognizes Adam's tyranny as injustice and immediately and decisively resists it ("I will not lie beneath you"). She is willing to take risks for her integrity and to relinquish a life of security in the Garden of Eden in order to uphold it, and she accepts uncomplainingly the consequences of her decision.

Only at the end of the story is there an O. Henry twist: She is referred to as a demon. This instantly converts all of these attributes, which may have seemed positive to women, into negative ones. But still, the unavoidable implication is that had her struggle for equality with Adam succeeded, she would not have had to leave him and become a vengeful and dangerous creature.

Jewish tradition is replete with folktales that have female endings when told by women and male endings when recounted by men (as well as some for both genders). The female folktales were transmitted orally, the ones with the male endings were generally written down. What may have happened with the Lilith story in the *Alphabet* is this: the core of the story may have been a folktale told by women to women over many generations, a story praising women's assertiveness under adverse conditions that had brought it to the fore. The author of the *Alphabet* may have cribbed this female story and added a negative ending, making it into a male story (or, more probably, one directed at both genders).

The purpose for the negative O. Henry twist at the end is to flip Lilith from positive to negative role model. Her refusal to be subservient ("I will not lie beneath you") and her escape from Adam provoked too much anxiety in the men to allow this behavior to stand. A woman who "withholds herself" from a man—either by refusing to be subservient or by denying him her very presence, thereby committing the great crime in Jewish life, abandonment—is a role breaker and must be transformed into a creature who is innately evil/demonic. (The anxiety about emotional abandonment is also behind the charge of Lilith's "frigidity" in the demon legends.)

The misogynist demon stories, written by men several hundred years after the *Alphabet*, reflect an intensified anxiety about Jewish survival and about the men's ability to ensure it. This anxiety is at the root of the specific crimes the stories attribute to Lilith: She is a slayer of babies and injurer of their mothers—thus threatening the physical survival of the Jewish nation. She also commits crimes against men: She steals sperm from them. By sapping the men's "life fluid" while they are asleep—a metaphor for reducing them to powerlessness—she weakens their ability to function as men; that is, she damages their masculinity. By thus impairing them psychologically, she impedes their ability to fulfill their role as men in ensuring Jewish survival.

It is not surprising that men's anxiety about Jewish survival should be expressed in late medieval stories since, as we have seen, the High Middle Ages were extremely lethal for Jews in Western Europe. The men's anxiety about their ability to ensure Jewish survival, however, is not expressed directly. That would have involved questioning the logic of the gender division of labor they had established. Given that the women's rates of conversion were lower than the men's during this period (and that in the Marrano era, women endured the tortures of the Inquisition with more fortitude than men), the implication would have been that perhaps men were not, after all, the gender best qualified for the job of spiritual resistance. The men, therefore, projected their anxieties about fulfilling their role onto the women, as represented by Lilith. It is the women, not the men, who are depicted as having the power to derail Jewish survival by not fulfilling *their* role.

Seen as a totality, the Lilith myth transmits the message that if a woman refuses to be an altruistic enabler, if she selfishly chooses independence over subservience, she will destroy the man's masculinity at a time when he has already been reduced to powerlessness. He will consequently not be able to play his role in advancing Jewish survival.

By making an independent woman a destroyer of Jewish manhood and Jewish lives, and an ally of the Jews' worst foe, who blocks Jewish liberation, the Lilith libel clearly tells us that *nothing less than Jewish survival hinges on the woman's behavior*: Jewish men will lose their manhood and the Jewish nation will consequently be destroyed if Jewish women refuse to stay in the subservient enabler role.

As if this warning were not enough, the authors of the demon tales of Lilith made sure to emphasize again and again her specific crimes against women. As baby slayer and mother injurer, she posed a danger to them at a time when infant mortality was high and the death of mothers in and after childbirth was common. Here Lilith is the flip side of the midwives in Egypt, who disobeyed the genocidal orders of the Pharaoh to kill the newborn boys and instead, the Midrash relates, took special care of them and their mothers. By picturing Lilith as a threat to individual women who were carrying out their prescribed wife-and-mother enabler role under difficult conditions, the male authors were attempting to keep them away from assertive women role breakers; just like the anti-Semites who created

Judeophobic myths, attempting thereby to keep oppressed non-Jews away from Jews. This divide-and-conquer technique was also designed to mobilize women to keep possible troublemakers in line by pitting "good" women against "evil" ones.

The Lilith myth tells us something even more chilling. In the gynophilic core of the story in the *Alphabet*, Lilith upholds the Jewish values at the heart of spiritual resistance in demanding mutuality in her relationship with Adam. Moreover, in arguing with him, she provides intellectual substantiation for her opinion as talmudic scholars do: with evidence from life experience ("We were both created from the earth").

When this approach fails, she forsakes the economic security of the Garden of Eden and accepts exile from society and a pariah status. In resisting oppression, in being highly conscious of her equality, in accepting outsider status in order to maintain her integrity, she behaves much like . . . the Jews! In fact, when she flies off from Eden, it is to the Red Sea, the precise scene of the Jews' consciously elected transition from the oppression and security of their bondage in Egypt to the insecurity and risks of freedom in the desert.

In her subsequent demonic incarnation, Lilith becomes a metaphor for the general societies of the Exile, which show different and sometimes contradictory "faces" to Jews, and all of which ultimately threaten their survival. The faces are the three strategies of oppression: the club, the yoke, and the leash.

The "club" strategy is annihilation: Lilith the baby slayer and mother injurer destroys the nation's continuity of generations and thus its future. Significantly, the men are not able to protect "their" women and children from Lilith's mayhem any more than they could defend them against rape and pogroms in the Exile.

The "yoke" strategy is the reduction of Jews to slavelike powerlessness—being the "king's persons" with the status of chattel and, in this and other ways, being forced to act in the interests of the rulers, not their own. Lilith saps men's "life fluid," a metaphor for power. In the context of medieval Europe, this is also a metaphor for draining the Jews' economic resources (one recalls here Abraham's description of them as "sponges" for the king).

The "leash" strategy of deceit is that of assimilation: Lilith is seductive but frigid, alluring but unresponsive to the man's psychological need for emotional support, and she ultimately abandons him.

Assimilation (which in the Middle Ages took the form of conversion) is seductive; it extends but ultimately withholds the brass ring of acceptance, as the Spanish conversos, Jews who became "New Christians" in the fourteenth and fifteenth centuries, learned. The nations to which Jews were so attached did not reciprocate their love and devotion (the Jews, who adored Spain, were summarily expelled in 1492).

Ultimately all three "faces" of the demonic Lilith, all three strategies of oppressive exiles, are variations of one: the face of the enemy working against, preventing, and/or delaying national redemption, the face of the "consort of Samael."

By juxtaposing these two images—Lilith as Exile, Lilith as Jew in Exile—we come to the true meaning and message of the Lilith libel: A Jewish woman who behaves in relation to a man in the courageous, independent-minded, unyielding ("stiff-necked") way that the Jewish nation behaves in relation to the general societies of the Exile is advancing the interests of those who wish to destroy Jewish identity, derail Jewish survival, and block Jewish liberation.

A woman behaving as a Jew in the community—who takes upon herself the role of ensuring Jewish survival by engaging in spiritual resistance (the way Lilith did at the onset)—is acting not in the interests of Jewish survival but of national destruction (as Lilith does later, when she shows her true demonic colors). If she is a "good Jewish daughter," she will not try to be a "real Jew." She will not engage in the study of Torah, as Beruriah did, or in the public performance of ritual, as some prominent medieval women did, because such participation will undermine the men's definition of masculinity (sap their "life fluid") and thereby render them psychologically incapable of engaging in this spiritual resistance work designed to ensure Jewish survival. Instead she must accept exclusion from this turf and adhere to the prescribed role of subservient, altruistic enabler. If she refuses to be an enabler, she flips over to the shadow role: disabler and enemy of the Jewish nation.

3
Lilith at the Red Sea

Sue D. Burton

It's a very strange legend. A woman runs away from a rapist and is told by her father—or a judge, or God, however you want to see it—to go back. "Or else."

She doesn't go back. The "or else" goes into effect—she's condemned to become a demon and to give birth to hundreds of children. And every day she has to watch these children die.

What's even more bizarre is that the woman herself doesn't question her father's curse. She says she has an agreement with him, a *covenant*: to live in a wasteland, obsessed with demons, and in return, to kill human babies.

In return? This is a pact with her father? What kind of story is this?

Now this is no ordinary woman. She knows her father's ineffable name, his magic, secret name. (A name, incidentally, that eons later his sons were still begging to hear.) She cries this name when she flees from the Garden where the attempted rape occurred.

Indeed, she does know her father's secret self, his "dark side." When he's angry and depressed, she becomes his consort.[1] Yes, she is called "harlot" or "bad daughter," but her father takes her as his consort when his "good daughter" is out of the house. But more of that later.

---

1. *Zohar* 3:69a.

The woman's name is Lilith. Some scholars say she was once a Goddess, in a time prior to the Garden in Genesis. They say this strange tale of Lilith fleeing the Garden is an explanation of an actual event—the invasion of an ancient queendom by nomadic herdsmen. When the queen flees, she's replaced with an agreeable shepherd girl—Eve.[2] Then the old queen is turned into a monster in the victors' war stories. It's like somebody's husband's stories about his first wife. What's really strange is how we keep falling for them.

* * *

I've struggled with Lilith for years. Ever since I heard her "alternative" Creation story, I've been obsessed, reading everything I could get my hands on. I can quote Patai on Lilith as a deposed fertility goddess, Scholem on Lilith as a projection of men's fears, Cantor on the historical context for the legends (most developed in Exile, when Jewish survival was at stake, when any woman who refused the role of "enabler" was a threat).[3]

Then there's the Kabbalah on the particulars of Lilith's femme fatale getup—scarlet dress, long red hair, flames from the navel down.[4]

I once spent months sorting through my hodgepodge of notations—I now have two milk crates stuffed with file folders: A to Z, *Alphabet of Ben Sira* to *Zohar*.

Over the years what I haven't been able to do is write a coherent piece on Lilith myself. I have stacks of unfinished poems (mostly about failed relationships and distant fathers). I have a play combining my experiences working at a women's health center with the story of Lilith at the Red Sea (a three-hour marathon with a cast including an abortionist, an anti-abortion picketer who—true story—comes into the clinic for an abortion, a white lesbian separatist as Lilith, and a black lesbian as the midwife Miriam whose loyalties are torn between Lilith and her brother Moses).

My most recent try was a short story in which the character Louise is explaining Lilith, Miriam, and *gilgul* (transmigration of

---

2. Robert Graves and Raphael Patai, *Hebrew Myths* (New York: Greenwich House), p. 69.
3. Aviva Cantor, "The Lilith Question," *Lilith* I, No. 1 (Fall 1976).
4. *Zohar, Sitre Tora*, 1:48 a–b.

souls) to her 82-year-old Lutheran mother as they drive to the grave of an aunt who (family secret) died in 1902 of an illegal abortion—and in the process, an old rift between mother and daughter is healed.

Got the picture? My latest thought is to pretend to be a Jungian analyst so I can write about my analysand who keeps spewing out demon children.

I know there's a reason for the demon children. In each of my ill-fated attempts, the question that's driven me is, how can Lilith be redeemed? I know I'm asking about myself. But I'm not sure what it means to be redeemed. And I'm not altogether sure what I have to be redeemed from.

* * *

In the beginning, in the very beginning, was Mother Sea. Chaos. An ocean of blood that gave birth to every living thing. Cultures all over the world have names for the Sea Goddess—you've probably heard of Aphrodite or Yemaya or Miriam. The Babylonian Great Womb was Tiamet.

Tiamet created the universe from her menstrual blood. Its reservoir was the Red Sea. In one version of the legend, she became a "dragon of chaos" killed by her own son. He split her corpse (her waters), just as in the Hebrew myth Moses divided the Red Sea.[5]

Tiamet was later known as Lilith.

* * *

Lilith lives outside the bounds of civilization, in the desert by the Red Sea. She's lonely. She's angry. Her demons are howling. She's turned herself into an owl, all feather and bone, anorexic.

She's rid herself of the garden—where trees grew behind fences and all the animals were named—yet she keeps on birthing demons. She can't stop spitting them out. It's as if her body is out of control. As if it isn't her own.

She obeys her father after all.

* * *

---

5. Barbara Walker, *The Women's Encyclopedia of Myths and Secrets* (San Francisco: Harper and Row, 1983), pp. 998–999.

Don't get me wrong. Lilith loves her demon children. Every one is precious. Every little aberration. Even the fetuses with wings. Even the ones whose hearts are disconnected from their lungs. Or whose lungs are all closed off.

And then the next one comes along.

It sounds like self-sabotage. But if the relationship is precious, why would she want to change it?

* * *

The daughter is furious at her father. He only heard Adam's side of the dispute. He didn't hear her terrified cry. Now she won't tell him how angry she is. She acts it out on other men.

She makes forays at night from her desert barricade and attacks the boundaries that weren't respected for her. She climbs into men's beds. She makes them spill their dreams. She spooks their pregnant wives. Best of all, she leaves her little demons in human baby bassinets. No one even notices their talons.

* * *

Lilith is the wife who flew off in a rage, but whose scent won't wash off the sheets.

* * *

The *Zohar* says Lilith is the mother of the "mixed multitude." Once, with Moses as their leader, this mixed multitude fled slavery in Egypt. Pursued by the Egyptian Pharaoh, they escaped through the clotted walls of the Red Sea just in the nick of time.[6]

This is the story that never gets told at Passover:

One day, just like any other day, Lilith is sitting by the Red Sea. Screech owl, she sits by the sea and shrills, the sound of talons scraping stone.

But that day she spies a cloud of dust advancing toward her through the desert. It's her changelings! The ones she'd left in Hebrew cribs.

At the head of the motley pack is Moses. Thick-necked Moses. Not one of her favorites.

---

6. *Zohar* 1:276, Exodus 12:38, Numbers 11:4.

Lilith flies over to Moses. He brandishes his rod.
Show your mother some respect, she screeches. *And you'd better be careful with that rod! I'll turn it into a snake.*
Moses strikes the Red Sea.
This is my blood, Lilith shrieks. *It answers only to me.*
Then Lilith sees on the edge of the sea Miriam, the midwife—the sister of Moses, who at her Hebrew mother's bidding, had once hidden the baby Moses in the Red Sea.[7] Miriam, the poet, who can still feel on the tips of her fingers the moist papyrus she'd woven into an ark delicate as paper, who can still see tiny ripples like endless spirals brushstroked on Egyptian waters, who smells the ginger of Egyptian thighs, who hears the clinking of bangles as the baby Moses is cradled in Egyptian arms.

Miriam, the prophet, who even this day tastes the salt of her mother's tears.

Suddenly the Pharaoh and his army are hurtling across the desert. Miriam covers her face.

And Lilith makes a path for her children.

* * *

Even though Lilith foresaw her daughter's fate, she opened the Red Sea.

Lilith knew that one day Miriam would question her brother. And that for this, God himself would call her a leper and cast her into the desert for seven days.

Lilith saw that Miriam, who as a 5-year-old had spoken audaciously to the Pharaoh,[8] would come out of the desert and never utter another word.

What was Miriam's crime? She spoke against Moses for turning his wife Zipporah away, for choosing celibacy over relationship. She sympathized with Zipporah, and with the wives of the other prophets who were following Moses' example.

So Miriam was punished—though as a child she'd been praised for convincing her father to remarry her mother. (Her father had

---

7. Louis Ginzberg, *The Legends of the Jews* (Philadelphia: The Jewish Publication Society of America, 1909), 2:265.
8. Ibid., pp. 251–252.

divorced her mother to avoid having boy children who might be destroyed by the Pharaoh. The remarriage resulted in Moses' birth.)[9]

And how did Lilith feel at the Red Sea when Miriam led the women in song praising God for delivering them?

* * *

Only once did Lilith let herself fly close to the circle of women. Only once did she cry, *Can't you see me?*

* * *

Lilith is the uninvited guest. The thirteenth fairy. The girl who just can't dance.

But that day by the Red Sea, Lilith began to dance. Even as she remembered the curse that had brought her to this place, she began to dance. Even as she foresaw her awkward steps as futile, she lifted her mud-caked claws and sang with all her might, screeching at the black sky, Miriam!

* * *

For years I've looked for a clue to Lilith's redemption in the Book of Isaiah. It's the only book of the Scriptures where she's mentioned, in 34:14, as the screech owl who lives among brambles and thorns.

Isaiah says one day the desert will blossom as the rose.

Interestingly, in the view of Isaiah II (yes, there's more than one—even prophets can have split personalities), the Creation and the Exodus are the most decisive events in the history of Israel. As we've seen, these are events in which Lilith has been intimately involved.

Isaiah II recounts the story of the crossing of the Red Sea using imagery drawn from the conflict between the Dragon Tiamet (Lilith)—sometimes called "the Deep"—and the Creator. (The Hebrew word for deep—*tehom*—is equivalent to the Babylonian word for Tiamet.)

Of course, in Isaiah's version, it's God Who makes a way for the redeemed to pass over the depths of the sea.

But Isaiah also says blessings from the Deep lie in wait below.

---

9. Ibid., p. 262.

Isaiah introduces the concept of the Suffering Servant, later developed in Jewish teachings as the Suffering Messiah or the Leper Messiah. The Suffering Servant (sometimes identified with Israel herself) is described as despised and forsaken, and acquainted with disease: "Although he had done no violence, and no deceit was in his mouth, yet it pleased the Lord to crush him by disease."[10]

Whereas Israel despairs, whereas she rebels and seeks vindication, the Servant "opened not his mouth," suffering patiently, for the sins of others.

Like a child, I've pored over Second Isaiah, trying to find a way to include Lilith among the redeemed. I've read and reread the passages about the forsaken woman from whom God hid his face only for a moment, "in a little wrath." The barren woman, the desolate children—all are to be redeemed. I'd say to myself, this means *everyone*, doesn't it?

But I can't make it work. Lilith would still have to beg for forgiveness.

* * *

Isaiah says the desolate children will be redeemed through a sin offering—the sacrifice of the messiah.

What if there was no sin?

* * *

I'm sitting here surrounded by notes from my Lilith/Incest file.

Here's Karen's paper and her Incest-Delinquency model—it all fits Lilith: excessive control by the father, labeling of the daughter as a whore, a sense of alienation from her family and the community, low self-esteem, acting out by engaging in *crimes* such as running away, substance abuse, and prostitution.[11]

In the margin by the I-D model are comments from my writers' group: these things also happen to women who assert themselves.

Here's a letter from Shirley and a handout about "psychological incest" she got at a speakout. "Incest can occur through an emotion-

---

10. Raphael Patai, *The Messiah Texts* (Detroit: Wayne State University Press, 1979), pp. 13–14, p. 17.
11. Karen Edwards, "Female Delinquency and Incest," Paper, National Council of Family Relations, San Francisco, October 1989.

ally suffocating, confusing relationship where a child is used to meet the sexual or sexual/emotional needs of a person in a position of trust or authority with that child."

And here's another reference to Lilith as God's consort brought into the temple, "the bridal chamber," then cast out. And a note on understanding redemption in sexual terms, in the erotic language of the *Zohar*—where everything is seen from the view of the striving male. And a quote from a biblical scholar who lists dire and numerous scriptural warnings against marriage between relatives and then notes, "It is surprising that marriage of a man with his daughter is not mentioned, and it must be presumed to have slipped out of the text."[12]

Indeed. But what do I do with all this? I don't want to understand redemption in sexual terms. Not when it leaves Lilith in a bridal chamber at the mercy of her father's whims.

Why do I have to take it all so literally?

* * *

I try so hard to be the good daughter. And to forget the rest.

* * *

They wandered, sun-struck and starving, in the desert near the Red Sea. And they lusted for the melons and leeks they'd left behind.

It had never been home. But they had such a yearning to go home.

* * *

Part of Lilith's pact with her father is that she won't cause harm to women in childbirth if they warn her away. She made a promise to respect amulets and incantations and magic circles. She only does her work if she's let in.

When Lilith comes to Miriam in the desert, she sees that Miriam had drawn a circle around herself. Miriam is crying. Her skin is as white and cratered as the moon. Lilith takes her place outside the circle beside the prophet Elijah.

---

12. Alan Richardson, *A Theological Word Book of the Bible* (New York: Macmillan, 1963), p. 139.

Why Elijah? He's always present at births. That's why a place is set for him at Passover.

Besides, he says, wrinkling his nose, (Tradition has it Lilith gives off a terrible stench!) *It's my job to ease tensions with the father.*

This is a mother-daughter deal, Lilith says. *Get lost.*

Miriam doesn't look up.

Now, now, Elijah says. *In no time you'll be a real beauty! Your husband will love it! In fact, I bet the two of you will end up great-greats to the Messiah!*

Miriam, Lilith says. *Let Mother fix you. Remember that morning I cured the Pharaoh's daughter? Remember how she stepped into the Red Sea and her nasty boils went right away?*

Pharaoh's daughter! Elijah snorts. *One of those moon worshipers. Just like Moses' wife.*

Lilith folds her wings over her chest. *Moses is afraid he might get burnt. By a little bush!*

And so it went—Elijah claiming that Miriam had to learn her lesson, that she had spoken up for lust, Lilith screeching that Moses was scared of his own shadow.

In the end Miriam heard the cry of a baby. And she went back to her family who'd waited for her those seven days.

Lilith got in the last word. *Then I'll be a great-great-great!* But Elijah had already disappeared. And she berated herself for not telling her daughter she understood it wasn't fair.

* * *

Miriam's crime was that she tried to fix the family. She "spoke directly" to Moses, for which she was chastised. Didn't she know anything about the rules of dysfunctional families?

Some people claim if you say you don't like something, if you express it decently, in a human way, then only an inhuman person wouldn't accept it. But if a family rests on silence, how can you ever say, *I don't like this?*

If by speaking the truth, the child is turned into a leper, then her father is inhuman—or the child is forced to invert reality. To say, *there must be something wrong with me.*

The problem is how do you tell if it's the other person, or if you haven't done it right? And right by whose terms? Aren't daughters more likely to blame themselves than call their fathers inhuman monsters?

Anyway, the formula doesn't always work. It didn't for Miriam. Of course, you could argue—and the argument has been made—that Miriam was a "tale bearer," acting out of jealousy, either of Moses' power or of his wife Zipporah herself. So you could say her resistance wasn't decently expressed. But then that leads into blaming the victim. *She didn't do it right. If only I'd done it right.* Etc. It's a losing battle.

Miriam lost on another front as well. That she and the women sang apart from the men at the Red Sea was later used to justify the segregation of the sexes in the synagogue.

Even the simplest things can become unbearably complicated.

* * *

What pact have I made with my own father?

* * *

Every day when I go in to work at the clinic, the picketers run toward me, yelling, *don't kill your baby!* It always takes them a few moments to recognize me. Then they shout, *Murderer! Witch!*

Walking past them, I'm as serene as the Virgin Mary, reciting under my breath my own litany: *Enjoy your ignorance while you have it!*

But sometimes I wonder about my own abortions.

I think about my parents. My mother, eaten up by anger. Her years of depression. Her screaming rages, her paranoia. And my father—what feelings I have for him are so buried, I've repressed the date he died. My few memories are of childhood injustices. Canceling my sleepovers with friends because mom was sick. That sort of thing. And the terrible feeling there was more, things I can't remember.

Have I been so afraid of repeating the cycle that I simply put a stop to it?

Now that I'm menopausal, I can let myself say, it doesn't have to be that way. Now that it's safe, I can finally say, I would be a good mother.

But I remain only a daughter.

4

A Midrash on the Creation of Woman

Elaine R. Barnartt-Goldstein

When Lilith heard her ex-husband had remarried, she was understandably jealous and curious to see the new wife. She decided to return to the Garden of Eden and hide so as not to have to speak to Adam, but in a place where she could see Eve. As it happened, she picked the very day when Eve took the apple from the Tree of Knowledge. As Lilith watched, the sin and discovery took place. When she heard the announcement of the punishment, she felt so sorry for the two of them that she jumped up from her hiding place and confronted God, saying:

"You are the Judge of the universe. Will You do so unjustly? You are punishing not only these two, who broke Your commandment, but also all the future generations, who did not."

God acknowledged her point and said, "In future generations, I shall make Adam's work fulfilling, and I shall cause medical science to begin so that Eve's daughters may be given anesthesia for their pain."

Lilith was not satisfied, but she was pleased that at least God had listened to her. She felt that the woman was still being punished more than the man and resolved to watch as the generations unfolded, visiting civilization from time to time to observe the treatment of women.

Lilith visited Sarai and Abram in their time. She noticed that

Abram was knowledgeable about God and protected by God, so she stayed with them, traveling as they did. When she overheard Abram asking Sarai to lie so that she might be raped rather than Abram murdered (Genesis 12:11–13), Lilith cried out to God.

"Lord, what a cruel and selfish man You are protecting! He is kinder to his nephew than to his wife. What will his punishment be?"

God answered, "Abram is destined to father My chosen people."

"Shall not the Judge of the universe do justly?" Lilith responded, using the line that had succeeded before.

God apologized then to Lilith and to Sarai and said, "I will require success on ten trials before Abram can father My people, and I will not allow any man to molest Sarai."

So Lilith had to be satisfied, and Sarai agreed to do as Abram asked. Abram was so impressed with Lilith's argument and its success, that he used the same words later to save Lot when God announced Sodom and Gemorrah's destruction.

Some time later, Lilith came to the Middle East and saw a group of men writing while God watched. She asked what they were doing and God answered that they were recording God's Talmud.

Lilith, invisible, read over their shoulders. She returned to God and said, "Lord, it sounds as though Your Talmud outlaws women's studying Your word, seeking justice in a courtroom, and divorcing their husbands. Will this document go through the centuries as Your people's truth?"

"Lilith," God answered, "The Talmud reflects the extent to which these men know Me. The women of this age have sinned against Me by asking their husbands to tell them what is ultimately true, rather than seeking Me themselves. They and their daughters are therefore punished by having to submit to laws made by men."

"But, God of Justice," said Lilith, "not all the women even of this age have sinned in that way. Beruriah and what's-her-name, Rabbi Akiva's wife, are seeking their own and the men's enlightenment. For their sakes, do not let this punishment be eternal."

God listened to Lilith and, for the sake of the holy women, decreed, "Though My Talmud will stand as written, in a hundred generations, women will earn an equal place in all aspects of Jewish life."

Lilith left the holy place impatiently. After 1500 years, she decided to be sure the history of women proceeded as she felt it should.

She visited the homes of Jewish women, inspiring them to study and to increase their independence. Then, toward the end of the hundred generations, Jewish women took up the cry, "Shall not the Judge of the universe do justly?"

5

The Lilith Poems

Alicia Ostriker

for Enid Dame and Grace Paley

1. Lilith To Eve: House, Garden

I am the woman outside your tidy house
   And garden, you see me
   From the corner of your eye
In my humble cleaning lady clothes
Passing by your border of geraniums
And you feel satisfied
You feel like a cat on a pillow

I am the woman with hair in a rainbow
Rag, body of iron
I take your laundry in, suckle your young
Scrub your toilets
Cut your sugar cane and
Used to plant and pick your cotton
In this place you name paradise, while you
Wear amulets and cast spells
Against me in your weakness

I am the one you confess
Sympathy for, you are doing a study
Of crime in my environment, of rats
In my apartment, of my
Sexual victimization, you're raising money

To send my child to summer camp, you'd love
If I were not so sullen
And so mute

Do you know my name
Do you know my name
Honey, do you know my NAME?

Catch me on a Saturday night
In my high heels stepping out and you shiver
I have the keys to your front door
In my pocket

2. Lilith Jumps The Fence

Girl, that man of yours
Was one pathetic creature
Puffing his chest, thinking the world of himself,
Standing there saying *Lie down* and *hold still*,
Waving his scepter at the jacaranda,
The bougainvillea, like the boss of something,
Though wasn't he only taking orders
From a bigger boss,
Or pulling stones from the ground to set on top
Of other stones, he'd say *We need this wall*,
Paradise constantly in
Motion, and him wanting it to stop—
What kind of husband
Was that, what kind of lover?

Honey, I answered
No hard feelings, but I don't like men
Who try to lay down the law
And I don't like enclosures
Nobody gives me orders
Now or ever

They say he invented names, and it's true
He called me shrew, bitch, witch,
and dumb cunt, he was that scandalized
Spilled a mouthful of curses
When I jumped that fence
Then God put him to sleep and gave him you

3. Lilith Deconstructs Scripture

And God saw that
You were go/o/d and

Told him your name
Was wom/b/an, a flesh
Section
A man/made
Abject object
Of his affection

Told him your name
Be quiet

You don't know you have   Eve
This curse, discourse
You are a mother
Tongue
The cause, the-
Ology the pre-
Text, the testament a
Testicle
To protect it is
Logical

                      you don't know you have
                      you are a mother
                      tongue

Let us be object/ive:
To hate, to penetrate
To legislate, and to
Enumerate, that is his
Temporary fate:

What's the appeal   *you m/other*
Of the apple: *of all living*
Take a bite, take a   *might   re/member*
Byte
And find out?

4. Lilith Unveils Herself

He thinks me evil, he be
Afraid of me and always desiring me

Chasing my black behind and my woolly black hair
But it's you I'm after,
Girl,
In the dark when I slip between
The two of you, whispering and touching
Laughing in your ear, I know
The man causes you pain but you stay faithful,
The man is boring but you pay attention,
The man some cardboard heart and you a mother
Watching your children hurt one another

I know
How you feel, I bear a hundred
Babies every day, and they die by nightfall
The man tells you to call them
Demons, to him it is nothing if they die,
But every midnight I kiss
Their dead faces
And then I creep into your house
With my smell of ripeness
With my smell of corpses, with my
Ancient angers
You feel me squeeze between you and the man
I hug your body, girl, I breathe
Have courage

5. Lilith Says Where Trees Come From

Changing the language is
Not easy you don't
Just disrupt
It you got
To raise it, raise it up but
What with?/ what with the
Weeds pushing
Busting with lust
Up between the cement
Cracks of our dirty sidewalks and what with
Their perfect stems and leaves their
Grace their goings
To seed and the stone
Crumbling up some more then

Overview: Who Is Lilith?

Pretty soon soil appears on
Some kind of time-scale
Which is not our business
How long it
May happen to take?/just
We keep pushing
Child, we keep dropping
The seeds

And being part of mystery that is
Bigger than language
And changes the language
And bursts it apart
And grows up and
Wildly away out of it

6. Lilith's New Song

Now clap your hands for this new song
Now sing it—
Here she comes
Yemanja
Here she comes
Seboulisa
Here she comes
Oshun
Here she comes
Inanna
Here she comes
Astarte
Here she comes
Ishtar
Here she comes
Kali
Here she comes
Gaia
Here she comes
Shekhinah
Here she comes
Mary
Here she comes
Spider Lady

Queen of Heaven and Earth
Queen of Ocean and
Big Queen of the Underworld
Now sing it
Now sing it
Ooooweeee
Doowaa
Shoobadoo-oo
Now clap those hands
And stamp those feet
And sing it!

6
Lilith's Version
Joanne Seltzer

In the second phase
of the beginning
God made me a gift
of an Adam doll
with visible
genitalia
& said *woman,*
go for a walk
in the apple grove
& said *woman,*
there's a snake charmer
I want you to meet
& said *woman,*
this is your last chance
to be a mensch.
Then God created
a different partner
for the Adam doll,
the pliant rib
who has been cloned
for generations
while I remain
the abstraction
of the beginning.

7

Strange Bedfellows: Holy Words and Demonic Images

(an excerpt)

Jo Milgrom

My purpose here is to take a single problem—the several meanings that grew out of a certain ambiguity in the biblical creation of woman—and follow that problem backward into the ancient Near-Eastern context and forward into the post-biblical Midrashic traditions. What will emerge from this combined study of literature with art will be an archetypal motif with a distinct, particularist point of view as it is filtered through the Jewish religious imagination.

Our point of departure, as might be expected, is Genesis 1:27–28, with its deliberate ambiguity:

27a And God created man in his own image,
27b in the image of God He created him.
27c male and female He created them.
28   God blessed them, saying, "Be fertile and increase, fill the earth and control it: rule the fish of the sea, the birds of the sky, and all the living things that creep on earth."

A close reading of v. 27 leads us to understand that 27b is a repetition of 27a, for emphasis, and that 27c is an appositive, spelling out that "him" is really plural, that the man *and* the woman were created simultaneously, and that both (v. 28) were to have dominion over the earth.

What, then, shall we make of Genesis 2:21–22, the better-known tale of the rib out of which Eve was formed?

2.21 So the Lord cast a deep sleep upon the man and he slept; and He took one of his ribs and closed up the flesh at that spot.

2.22 And the Lord God fashioned into a woman the rib that He had taken from man, and He brought her to the man.

Did the world begin with a menage à trois? Already another woman? If indeed Eve was second, who was first? Where did she come from and what happened to her? Long before her affiliation with Adam, long before the Bible and outside of its environment, the world of myths and demons knew her as Lilith, and her story recedes far back into human consciousness.

A Sumerian king list (circa 2400 B.C.E.) identifies the father of the great hero Gilgamesh as Lillu. Now Lillu was one of four demons belonging to a class of vampires or incubi-succubae (depending on their plumbing), ghostly night visitors who conceived or begot children by their human hosts. Lilith, female counterpart of Lillu, was believed to be harlot and vampire, never releasing her lovers or ever satisfying them.

Theologically promoting her from mere demoness to the pantheon, the earliest depiction of Lilith is a terra cotta relief set on a mountainous ledge, the ideal Mesopotamian religious landscape of the early second millennium. Naked and voluptuous, winged and taloned, she mounts a lion and is flanked by owls. She carries a menacing ring and staff, tools for measuring and limiting the span of man's life, or judging him at death. She wears the same empowering headdress and carries the same tools as the sun god on a stele showing Hammurabi receiving divine legal authority.

Whatever beliefs may have been alive concerning Lilith during Israel's first and second Temple periods, the Bible does not let on. What we do see in the Bible is the laconic and recurring evidence of a polemic against the fertility religion of the Canaanite inhabitants of the Land of Israel.

It is only later, in post-biblical Jewish literature, when the fear of paganism and the fear of idolatry were laid to rest, that the old mythology was allowed to surface; Lilith then turns up in the Talmud and Midrash, and at about the same time (300–600 C.E.) in incantation bowls found in Nippur, in Babylonia, where the Tigris and Euphrates come together, in an area thought to be Jewish. Turned upside down under the corners of rooms, under arches and thresholds, texts were found showing Lilith naked, with long loose hair, pointed breasts, no wings, strongly marked genitals, and chained ankles. Once attached to humans, these demons, both male and female, could only be expelled by divorce! Jealous of the human mates of their bedfellows and their children, they caused miscarriage, barrenness, infant mortality, childbed fever and death. . . .

What have we so far? To summarize: a monster, a demon, who has both feminine and masculine aspects, who at least in the feminine aspect has become a goddess. She personifies the dark side of feminine creative and sexual powers. She is not a wife, but a seducer; she is not faithful, but promiscuous. Even though sex produces life, she is a baby- and mother-killer. Thus she personifies the fear that resides in all of us. For women it is the fear that in bearing new life, they, the bearers, may not survive; and/or that the new life itself may not survive. The siren, a Greek version of Lilith, is a threat to men, representing their fears: loss of potency; loss of the nurture and devotion of a wife; loss of progeny (hence *immortality*, in the sense that children are one's immortality and continuity). . . .

The first inkling we have of Lilith's unusual character is that she goes to Egypt. Egypt is the seat of witchcraft. The name of the country, *Mizraim*, can be read *m'zarim*, "oppressors," "demons." As for the Red Sea, water is the abode of demons. Rachel Adler observes that her extravagant fertility begins as soon as she separates from Adam. At any rate, happy in her newfound freedom, Lilith refuses to come home—that is, until she hears about *Eve's* creation, at which point she plots her revenge.

II

LILITH AND MEN

Lilith and her twin brother had been free, strong, and joyous. They shared carefree adventures and sparkling sex together, sometimes going their separate ways and then rejoining. Suddenly he declares that she must obey him and acknowledge his mastery, whether in sexual position or intellectual decision.

She leaves. She learns to be free, strong, and independent. But, some of the writers in this section will say in varied ways, her independence is in reference to Adam. Sometimes she wants him back but not on his terms. Her history with him often infuses her later relationships with other males, whether men, demons, satyrs, or even God.

8
Adam

Grace Herman

When I feel alone
the air is full of demons
spitting spite and prophesies

You will die young
You will not die young
and your pain will go on and on

Lightheaded
not opening myself to silence
I weaken

and blame another
any other
Lilith for instance calling

her monster—night hag—
seductress (not so unhappy
about that)—goat scourge

gains me nothing
my second wife Eve wants to hear
none of it

9
Drifting Like Smoke

Barbara D. Holender

I know you better than you know yourself, he said,
defining me. Oh, he knew it all
but he knew it all wrong.
I know what you want, he said, giving me what he knew
I wanted, which was not at all what I wanted
but it was his gift.
I know what you need, he said, you need to be taken,
I will take you, drain you, I know what you need.
So I flew out through the corner of his eye
drifting like smoke above him.
Adam, I said, you give me your seed,
I am fat with it, but what grows in me
you will never know. And I gave him blossoms
of my body and smoke of my mind in forms
strange to him, so that all that he gave me turned
changeling. Now I hover out of reach watching him
peer here and there, shaking his head.
His new wife says yes dear, Thank you dear,
Of course dear. She feeds him wholesomely, accepts
his giving and his knowing, seeks herself in his eyes.
She too grows fat with his seed, but what she bears
resembles him. His little ones say YesDaddy
thankyouDaddyofcourseDaddy. All his knowing
is right where he can grasp it; yet how restlessly
he probes the earth, searches the sky.

10

Lilith

Enid Dame

kicked myself out of paradise
left a hole in the morning
no note no goodbye

the man I lived with
was patient and hairy

he cared for the animals
worked late at night
planting vegetables
under the moon

sometimes he'd hold me
our long hair tangled
he kept me from rolling
off the planet

it was
always safe there
but safety

wasn't enough. I kept nagging
pointing out flaws
in his logic

he carried a god
around in his pocket
consulted it like
a watch or an almanac

it always proved
I was wrong

two against one
isn't fair! I cried
and stormed out of Eden
into history:

the Middle Ages
were sort of fun
they called me a witch
I kept dropping
in and out
of people's sexual fantasies

now
I work in New Jersey
take art lessons
live with a cabdriver

he says: baby
what I like about you
is your sense of humor

sometimes
I cry in the bathroom
remembering Eden
and the man and the god
I couldn't live with

11
Lilith's Version

Ona Gritz-Gilbert

Bland paradise, Eden,
only sweet fruit growing on those trees.
Even the forbidden was waxy to the touch
and smelled . . . nutritious.
No poetry, I'd open up my mouth
and only niceties emerged.
The animals, with their wet, grateful eyes,
seemed bored.
I needed sweat and smoke;
I craved a change of weather,
the restless pull of an ocean.
I chose evolution,
it recognized the animal in me.
As for Adam,
he had a name for everything
except my leaving.
Jewelweed grew in the garden—
he called it impatiens;
that's the closest he came
to understanding me.

12
Male and Female Created He Them

Nikki Stiller

Even in Eden she envied him.
He always worked at the mountaintop,
she in the valleys; he kept to sunlight,
she preferred the shade. He was used

to adulation. To her it came seldom.
Her soul fluttered; his was as sleek
as a cat, as eloquent as an arrow.
She was pursued by her appetites,

he set out to subdue and tame them.
She did not like to fight; he was
always eager to win. Together
they lived apart, not in solitude,

exactly, but each one nursed a hurt
that could not be cured by talk.

And there sprang up two diverse nations
which still exist, unto this day.

13
Adam and Lilith, Adam's Eve

Henny Wenkart

Free and strong they came together
She and Adam, in the sweet cockcrow of youth
Aflame for one another, desirous, admiring
Keepers of one another's soul.

Later the staleness of his blood made a long backwash
Of bitter demons, began to call each demon Lilith
Labeled Lilith the bundle of regret, and rage, and her,
Shot the whole bundle into outer darkness.

"I want someone just like myself to cheer me
Rib of my side, my temperament and nature."
Out of such gossamer he now constructs his Eve
All lightness, all compliance and laughter.

No living woman is a man-imagined Eve or Lilith.
How did she turn into his nightmare or his dream?

14

The First Divorce

Mary L. Gendler

Once upon a time, long long ago, near the beginning of time, lived the first human couple, Adam and Lilith. Both had been newly created by the union of Earth and Sky, Adamah and Elohim, and since this was the time before all the trouble began, they found themselves, upon awakening from their unformed state, in a beautiful Garden filled with trees and fruit, friendly animals, and eternal warmth and sunshine. They awoke to find each other and awoke to each other, and in the beginning it was good. Since everything was provided for them in the garden and there wasn't much work to do, they got along well, playing like children and enjoying their surroundings and each other. It wasn't until Elohim asked Adam to name the animals that the trouble began.

"Why should you get to name all the animals?" Lilith complained. "I want to name some, too."

"He told me it was *my* job, so I'm going to do it, and that's that," retorted Adam. (Their first fight.)

After this angry exchange Lilith wandered off by herself and sat down under a slender fruit tree, nursing her confusion. After all, she, like Adam, had been birthed from the belly of Adamah, their mother. She, like Adam, had wandered around the garden, rejoicing in its beauties and wondering at the miracle of the creatures Elohim and Adamah had placed there. Her voice filled the space between earth and sky with words and music as did Adam's, and her curiosity and imagination were rich and boundless. Why, then, had Elohim singled out only Adam to name the animals? Had she done something wrong? She felt a terrible gnawing, filled-up feeling inside of her, a sensation she had never before experienced. Since she had no words for this feeling, she could not name it, but her heart felt weighted down, and to her amazement she felt drops of water falling from her eyes. These drops fell upon the ground, watering the roots of the tree that shaded and supported her, a tree that, later, was to be the center of much controversy.

When she arose, she wandered alone around the garden, silently naming the animals to herself.

This incident, unfortunately, marked the beginning of a long, painful struggle between Adam and Lilith. As the battles grew more fierce, they both longed for the days when they had enjoyed each other's company, whether it was strolling around the garden or making love. In those days it had been almost as if they were two complementary parts of a whole, so well they understood and matched each other. But they were caught in something else now, something they didn't understand. The more Adam tried to tell Lilith what to do, the more she resisted, and the further apart they grew. Indeed, they even began to look more and more different. Adam, whose features and body had had a certain sweetness and softness, began to grow hard and tough. He became preoccupied with the strength of his body, as if having a strong body would insure his supremacy over Lilith. He moved rocks around in the garden and insisted on doing all the hard work, "to protect Lilith." She, for her part, felt more and more distant from Adam. No longer wanting to be close to him, she began to resist his love advances.

The crisis came one night when Adam insisted that Lilith lie beneath him instead of side by side as had been their custom. When she protested, he said, "Look, I'm in charge here, so I'm going to be on top."

"Like hell you are!" yelled Lilith. "I'd rather leave than spend the rest of my life being bossed around by you."

"Sure," replied Adam mockingly. "Where do you think you'll go? Outside of this garden there is nothing but wild beasts and lava fields and desert. You'll never survive."

"Don't worry about me. I can take care of myself!" Lilith asserted bravely, although she was shaking inside. "I can do a lot of things you don't even know about. In any case, I'm leaving!"

And she did.

Adam was astounded. At first he didn't really believe her, but when he heard her utter the Ineffable Name, calling upon the One who contains all, the Great Parent of Elohim and Adamah, he knew she was serious. Powerless to stop or follow her, he watched helplessly as she disappeared before his very eyes.

"She'll be back before tomorrow night," he consoled himself. "She's afraid of the dark and she'll never be able to take care of herself out there."

But a week passed and she did not return. Adam alternated between fury and despair. Sometimes he imagined that she had been attacked and eaten by a wild beast, and he wept with sorrow. His beautiful, wonderful Lilith. How had this happened? What had gone wrong? Why had she done this to him? They had had a good life here. He had been kind to her and provided her with everything she needed. Why had she insisted on spoiling things? Why did she make such a fuss over the simple naming of the animals? And why wouldn't she let him protect her? Who was she, anyway? Thus he brooded.

Finally he decided to seek out Elohim.

"Elohim, I have a terrible problem. Lilith has left the garden."

Elohim was startled. He'd been so busy with the angels and other parts of his realm that he hadn't been paying much attention to the garden and his children recently. The last time he had looked in, the two of them had been happily romping with the other creatures in the garden. It was at that time he had whispered to Adam to name the animals. Somehow it seemed wrong that he had not gotten around to giving them names yet. Besides, Adam, though a lovely, charming boy, was still just that, a child, really, who took nothing seriously. He had given him the task in the hope that the responsibility might help him to mature, to take life a bit more seriously. It was to be his initiation into the more spiritual, intellectual realm, for to name something is to help shape its form and meaning.

How was he to know that Lilith would react this way? She had somehow always seemed more sensible than Adam, more rooted. Besides, Adamah had never insisted on doing everything he, Elohim, did. They had always had their separate realms. While he took care of the airy spheres and commanded the wind and sun, she was busy in her own arena, constantly giving birth to new forms and creatures, fecund and fruitful, explosive and gentle, unpredictable and, above all, exquisitely beautiful. Again and again he returned to her, fertilizing her with life-giving water, and embracing her with the sunny rays of his passion. And from their union sprang the myriad forms of life that now inhabited Earth.

What had gone wrong with Adam and Lilith? Elohim was truly puzzled. To Adam he said,

"Don't worry, son. I'll send my diplomatic angels after her. I'm sure they'll be able to talk some sense into her."

"That's wonderful," sighed Adam with relief. "I really miss her and I'm having trouble deciding what to eat. Anyway, she had no right to run off like that. I want her back!"

So Elohim sent his most trusted messengers, Gabriel, Raphael, and Uriel, to find Lilith. But this was not so easy. She had first returned to her mother, Adamah, for advice, and Adamah had listened to her story with sympathy and sadness.

She and Elohim had had a beautiful and peaceful relationship since the first moment the Ineffable, the Supreme One, had, in a moment of ecstasy, birthed them both at the same time and given them the charge to create a new Universe, one that would be alive with spirit, whose myriad creatures, large and small, rooted and nonrooted, would live in harmony, embodying and reflecting the glory of the Nameless One, the Glory of Being, the Wonder of Becoming. They had worked together on this charge, and their culmination, their most beautiful creation (in Adamah's opinion, though she knew she shouldn't play favorites) had been Adam and Lilith. And now Lilith had left Adam. What a tragedy!

She could understand her daughter's restlessness, this young woman who had never had the opportunities for creation that she had. No wonder she felt the need to assert herself, to find a meaning for her existence!

Lilith had come to her mother to receive her blessing. Adamah, though saddened, understood Lilith's need and freely granted her permission to wander throughout her dominion, blessing her daughter through her tears.

So Lilith wandered for many days until she found a spot that she felt was just right. She settled into a cave on the shores of the Red

Sea where she soon gave birth to seven beautiful babies, the fruit of an earlier union with Adam. By the time the angels found her she had become quite established in her new home. She was digging in her garden when Elohim's messengers arrived.

"Hello, Lilith," said Gabriel. "How are you managing all by yourself? And look, now you have all these children to care for in addition."

"You have to work so hard, digging a garden and creating everything from scratch. Why don't you come back to the Garden where all you have to do is just pick the food from the trees?" said Raphael sweetly.

The third angel, Uriel, took a different tack. "Adam is terribly lonely. He mopes around all day and doesn't know what to do with himself. He needs you."

Lilith continued digging while they were talking. "Why should I go back? He tells me what to do all the time. I'm doing fine. Tell him I'll come back only on the condition that we really share, that we co-operate on everything. If he agrees, I'll return. Otherwise, no!"

The angels, surprised by her firmness as by her success in establishing herself so well in the wilderness, tried their diplomatic best to convince her to return but to no avail. They returned to Elohim and Adam with the news.

Adam, upset to learn that she was doing so well, was furious at her message. "Who does she think she is? I know what will happen. I'll give in this time and then she'll want more. She'll be even harder to live with now that she's 'made it' out there. Anyway, I want my children! Do something, please, Elohim!"

Elohim, truly distressed himself by this time, tried to think of a solution. All he could think of was to try to force her to come back. He would first threaten her with permanent exile from the garden, and if she still refused he would threaten to take her children away from her. Surely this would frighten her into returning.

By the time the messengers returned, Lilith's garden had sprouted and her home had begun to resemble the Garden that she had fled . . . only this one did not have a wall around it.

Lilith was startled by the angels' pronouncements and more than a little frightened. To be on her own for eternity was a terrifying prospect. She loved the Garden and ached to see it again, but she knew, now, that she could never return. But what about the children? Would they really be taken from her? She couldn't bear that. For a moment, Lilith almost gave in, but the voice of her mother, Adamah, whispered in her ear:

"You are my daughter and I will not abandon you. Stay with me, live by me, and you will survive. I will feed you and provide you with shelter, warmth and safety. Do not be afraid."

"Tell Elohim and Adam that my answer is NO," said Lilith after a moment. "I can never return. And as for the children, tell Elohim that I will never allow them to be taken from me. I would rather see them die than live as masters or servants or eternal children!" She turned and slowly disappeared into the darkness of the cave.

The three messengers returned to Elohim and Adam and reported, "She refuses to come back."

Elohim and Adam were stunned.

"It looks like she's really gone," said Elohim.

"But what am I going to do? I need somebody!" wailed Adam.

"First of all, we need to recognize formally that this relationship is at an end," said Elohim. "So, as Supreme Judge, I will declare your union officially terminated, but to do so, we have to have a word for this. Adam, since you like to name things so much, you think of something. What shall we call it?"

Adam thought for a minute. "Let's call it divorce."

"Fine," said Elohim. "I now declare you and Lilith divorced. We'll see what we can do about getting your children back, but that may be difficult. Lilith seems very determined. Perhaps we should just get you another woman, one who won't be so assertive...."

"That's a great idea, Elohim. Thanks," said Adam.

15
Lilith's Divorce
Naomi Gal

The chief *dayan* studies her from his seat on high: "Your name is not a Jewish name," he says, "Lilith is the name of a demon. You must change it." The other two *dayanim*, who flank him, nod in agreement.

"I'm not here because of my name," Lilith says faintly and exchanges a glance with Adam. He shrugs, a small malicious smile flitting over his face.

"I believe that for the purpose of *shlom bayit* you must change your name," the *dayan* continues. The two bearded *dayanim*, one on his right and one on his left, continue to nod. "You should be happy that your husband is willing to take you back," says the *dayan* on the left, his beard so long that it sweeps the table in front of him.

Because of the beard Lilith thought he would be the nicest of the three. Now she changes her mind. "I don't want *shlom bayit*," she says courageously, defying her lawyer's advice; "I want a divorce. And he does, too," she says, and points to Adam.

All of a sudden it feels like a replay of the Lilith legend. Adam seems to her like Adam, the first man; she herself is Lilith, who has just pronounced the Name of God and vanished; while the three *dayanim* are Senoi, Sensoi, and Semangalaf, the three angels who were

---

* Translated from the Hebrew by Suzy Shabetai.

sent to bring her back to her husband. Lilith begins to laugh and notices the glance Adam exchanges with the three *dayanim*. Of course. Lilith is a demon, a harmful creature, and first and foremost an unbalanced woman. Lilith has a vision of herself with her tousled hair, long and seductive, her lips painted red, her eyes shooting sparks of anger. The *dayanim* will have something to fantasize about tonight, and someone to blame for a little nocturnal pollution, or if they turn to their wives with an unusual enthusiasm. She laughs, knowing that if she doesn't stop she will begin to weep hysterically; the three representatives of the Holy One, blessed be He, who sit high above her are about to settle her fate and the fate of her children. She tries to swallow her laughter but doesn't succeed; the situation seems so ridiculous to her.

"The woman will control herself!" orders the elder *dayan*, who sits in the middle. Lilith stops at once. She remembers what her lawyer told her: if you're not careful they'll give your husband custody of the children. If the *dayanim* conclude that she is unbalanced, she could pay the highest price of all. A price like that paid by the mythic Lilith for her refusal to return to her husband, Adam: she was sentenced to mate all night, every night, with demons and give birth every morning to a hundred stillborn babies. A shudder passes down Lilith's back. It's cold in the shadowy room; daylight barely penetrates the narrow window that is high up, almost on the ceiling, the glass pane so dirty that the rays of sunlight seem to be deflected from their paths in fear.

"Your husband is willing to forgive you and he agrees to turn over a new leaf," says the youngest *dayan* softly, who sits on the right hand of the chief *dayan*. Long black peyot move on either side of his head as he speaks. Lilith fastens her gaze on him, fascinated. "There are two young children in your home," he adds and looks straight into her eyes, unlike the other two *dayanim*. Lilith is first to look down. His gaze is too powerful. Or perhaps it only seems that way to her because of the shadows.

"For a long time the woman has behaved in an unseemly fashion, and she also neglects the home, her husband, her little children," the *dayan* reads from the petition; "the woman is a *moredet*, a rebellious wife, she does not follow religious precepts and does not reform her behavior, despite her husband's demands and warnings."

"He's the one who neglects the home!" Lilith flares up, "He

doesn't even live in the country!"

"I only went abroad to check out the possibilities, Rabbi; after all, I have to provide for my wife and children," says Adam in his most unctuous voice.

"He's on a sabbatical at Columbia University in New York," Lilith shrieks.

"Please," says the youngest *dayan*, "your husband is willing to try *shlom bayit*. He is willing to stay in Israel and be with you and your children."

"They're his children, too," Lilith says automatically, again forgetting the lawyer's instructions: don't say a word in the presence of the *dayanim*, unless they ask you a question.

"Of course, it would be better if you joined your husband in America," says the chief *dayan*. "A woman's place is beside her husband, and if your husband has to spend a year at a university abroad, you should be with him and keep a kosher Jewish home."

"But what about my career?" Lilith doesn't restrain herself, even though she can guess the response.

"I am sure you will find an occupation even in a strange place," says the *dayan* with the long beard. "A home and small children are a full-time job for a good wife."

"The house and family are like a small kingdom and there cannot be two kings wearing one crown," the chief *dayan* reads from the petition. "Many crowns are set aside for the woman at home," he glances at Lilith and enumerates them: "*Keter Bina, Keter Tiferet*, the crown of wisdom, the crown of beauty." He goes back to the petition and continues reading: "While *Keter Malchut* is for the husband's head," and he looks at Adam, who smiles from ear to ear. "Anyone who tries to change that law will render up his soul and bring evil on his family, he will turn aside goodness and lose his portion in the world to come, yet he will not change that law." The chief *dayan* bangs his hand on the table. "We ask you most earnestly, Mrs. Appel, to make an attempt at *shlom bayit* without putting obstacles in the way. The session is now at an end."

"But . . ." Lilith cries.

"No buts," Adam quickly says loudly, to distract her; "*shlom bayit* will work for us, I'll take responsibility," he tells the *dayanim*. He pushes Lilith outside, snapping: "Can't you see there are other couples waiting!"

Lilith seethes with anger. She looks at the dozen couples who have been waiting for hours for their session with the *dayanim*. "It's a waste of your time," she says to a middle-aged woman who is about to enter. "They'll be on his side anyway." Lilith indicates the man beside the woman, who is wearing a *kippa*. Adam shoots an apologetic glance at the crowd around the door of the court and continues to urge her out to the stairway.

"Don't touch me!" Lilith shrieks.

"I'm not touching you," says Adam, "and stop making a scene!"

"Don't worry, these walls have seen everything already," Lilith shouts. She hates the Rabbinate. She knew beforehand that the game was rigged. But, even so, she had hoped that Adam would soften, would agree to tell the *dayanim* that he wanted the divorce. Her lawyer warned her of the possibility that Adam would ask for *shlom bayit*. "He's piling up the credit points," he said, "while at the same time he's wearing you down. You have to be patient." Lilith can't be patient. She detests the sanctimonious *dayanim*; she can't understand how in a progressive country—which apparently isn't progressive at all—three representatives from the Middle Ages can settle her fate.

She stops and turns to Adam: "This is the late twentieth century," she says to him, "how can you allow those primitive types to decide what's going to happen to us?"

Adam gives his Machiavellian smile: "They're not deciding what's going to happen to us. You are." Lilith doesn't bother to ask him what he means. She has to go to her lawyer. Now, immediately. To tell him how the first meeting at the Rabbinate went. "What now?" says Adam with a smile. "Shall we go home to the Garden of Eden?"

"Go to hell!" says Lilith, turning her back on him and scooting down the stairs. She stops a cab at the Rabbinate entrance, gives the driver Sammy Almog's address, and starts to cry. "All the women who come out of that building cry," says the driver in a show of sympathy, "it makes a lot of trouble for people, that Rabbinate. Your husband wants a divorce and you don't?" Lilith shakes her head, but can't answer, she is weeping without restraint, feeling humiliated and beaten and mostly scared—for the first time since divorce proceedings started, she fears losing her children. Lilith gives the driver double the amount shown on the meter, but doesn't wait for her change and rushes straight into Almog's office.

Almog looks at the make-up smeared over her cheeks and her

disheveled hair; he sighs and says: "Don't tell me, I know. I told you so."

"You did. But I didn't imagine it would be that bad."

"It'll be worse if you don't start listening to me."

"I'm all ears," Lilith groans.

"They told you to go home and try *shlom bayit*?"

"Yes."

"Okay. As expected. Now you have to take off the kid gloves and start fighting."

"Whatever you say."

"The first thing is a restraining order forbidding him to leave the country."

"But..."

"No buts, Mrs. Appel. Unless you want to give everything up. And then there's no point in your paying me; you won't need a lawyer."

"All right. A restraining order stopping him from leaving the country. But it isn't fair, he has to go back to Columbia. His career depends on it."

"Great. Let's use that. We'll also freeze his bank account and all the savings accounts."

"But..." The lawyer ignores her protest.

Lilith tells herself that she is incapable of doing these dreadful things to anyone and certainly not to Adam; after all, he is the father of her children. "Look," she says weakly, "I'm willing to give up the house, the car, the savings, I don't mind, but not the children..."

"There's something you don't understand, Mrs. Appel. He doesn't want the children, I'm telling you, I know this game, I've made my living from it for twenty years. It's only a bargaining point, can you understand that? What's he going to do with the children in New York? Believe me, he's only using this because he knows you're prepared to give everything up if you can only keep the children."

"But he loves them..."

Sammy looks at his watch impatiently, "I wish I represented your husband instead of you. We'll lose, all because you insist on being nice. Divorce is a dirty game. There's no room for courtesy and consideration. It's you or him. You can't both win."

"I don't want to win... why should..."

"I'm the lawyer," says Sammy Almog and bangs his hand on his wide desk. Reminded of the identical gesture made by the chief dayan, Lilith is silenced. It's men's day today, she tells herself, I won't contradict them any more and I won't annoy them. They're the ones who decide. The only thing I can do is to sit and listen like a good little girl. Like a good wife. Even though to them I'm a bad wife. What did they call me? A *moredet*—a rebellious wife. She listens. She nods. She agrees to every word, even though her stomach is turning. She walks home. Slowly. Trying to put off the unavoidable meeting with Adam. Praying he won't be home. Her heart skips a beat when she goes into the house and discovers that the children aren't there.

Adam comes out of the shower and at the sight of her frightened face he gives that jeering laugh of his that she has come to hate. "I haven't kidnapped them yet," he says. "They're at my mother's." Lilith sinks into the couch, completely drained. Adam sits down opposite her and pours himself a generous shot of brandy.

"Adam," she says, trying to speak as quietly and nicely as possible, "why can't we get a friendly divorce? It seems that you just can't cope with my need for a life of my own, a career, and even less with my success."

"Success?" Adam gives his evil laugh. "You published two antireligious articles, which made a little splash. Let's not exaggerate. As I see it, you'd be a lot more successful if the children were happy and the house was clean and tidy."

"The children are fine, Adam. You're not. I want to make it clear to you: I'm not going to give up my career. And next year will be even harder because I intend to complete my postdoctorate studies at long last and I don't care what it takes."

"I don't care either," says Adam and takes a long swig of brandy, "I, let me remind you, am going to Columbia with or without you." He looks at her and adds in an ice-cold voice: "And the children are coming with me."

All of a sudden Lilith forgets Almog's warnings. She pounces on Adam like a wounded tigress. The brandy snifter is sent flying and smashes to pieces; she goes for his throat, but he shoves her away. She falls on the floor next to the couch, bruised, out of breath, wanting to throw herself on him again in a blazing rage to scar him, but Adam gets up, goes into the bedroom, puts on a sweater, picks up the car keys and leaves the house without saying a word.

Lilith remains lying on the floor, unable to move; it's only now that she sees that her arm was cut by the broken glass. She watches the blood flow, hating Adam with all her soul. She knows he won't be back that night, like all the other nights. She wishes he would die. "*Adonai Elohim Jahveh,*" she screams in defiance, like Lilith her predecessor, her progenetrix, and immediately feels an immense relief. A wave of freedom washes over her, carries her aloft, like a pair of enormous wings, and she knows that nothing can stop her journey. She knows the price she will have to pay. She is ready and willing.

16
Feminist Revaluation of the Mythical Triad of Two Women and One Man: Lilith, Adam, Eve

Henny Wenkart

Lilith refused the subservient role and since she, but not Adam—in a myth written down by men!—possessed the power of the ineffable name of God, she flew away by means of this power. Her "crime" is stubbornness, insubordination.

Contemporary feminists point out that since Lilith's origin is coterminous with that of Adam, she is never *subordinate* to him, hence cannot be accused of *in*subordination with any consistency. These women see Lilith as strong and independent always, a creative spontaneous source always. But in her relationships, what great and contradictory variety! She may be sisterly, motherly, amorous, or envious toward other women, depending upon the woman who dreams her. She may be indifferent to men, or sexually joyful and desirous of them. She may be childless or the mother of many. In confronting her successor wife Eve, she acts in some works as temptress and destroyer; in some as sympathetic and helpful sister; sometimes as benign maternal figure; other times as lesbian love, cuckolding Adam in collusion with Eve—or spitefully using Eve as a means of revenge.

Rebecca Milstein suggests that on the hermaphrodite model, Lilith's making love with Eve is not a cuckolding of Adam, but an incorporation of his love for Eve—since Lilith and Adam are one, literally one flesh. Interesting that while creating a new myth, these women find inspiration in seeing themselves as reinterpreting, or even restoring, the truth about an existing figure whose nature has been slandered by men. As successor to the ancient goddess Hinani, and later Ishtar, Lilith represented an aboriginal positive value of female freedom, power, spontaneity, and generosity.

In some of the poems and stories the image of flying, lightness, and strength predominates. Others stress gentleness-in-power, as symbolized in water images. Many assert a strong connection of femaleness with fertility blood. The common element is the assertion of woman as primary—where man appears, *he* is the "other."

The male principle is present in Lilith myths—as friend or as enemy. But present. When feminist writers see Lilith as independent, it is specifically of men that she is independent.

If Deborah Tannen is right, and most men see relationships as either one-up or one-down, then Lilith's striving for equality with Adam must come to grief: for if she were to achieve intimacy and equality with him, in his eyes he would have suffered defeat. A little boy may fear and resent his mother's power over him, which she exerts because of her larger size and strength, among other things. But he has power over her as well, because he can control her love button. As a man he is confronted by women who control his love button, his penis. As a teenager he must watch helplessly as this most intimate, sensitive part of his body rises up against his will under the influence of a female. Later in life she still exerts control there, when against his opposite willing, now it remains soft when he wishes it to rise hard and conquering, except if a woman—and often the wrong woman!—commands. But if woman has him in her power and control in this way, his only safety lies in controlling her in turn.

Woman also controls man's continuance into future generations, which must be hatched in her womb. The myth demonizes both Lilith's sexual attractiveness and her procreative power, turning these powers into destructive forms. She is said to interfere between spouses when they copulate, to cause a man to spill his seed through sexy dreams, to bring about mishaps in childbirth.

The male Midrash-makers of the Middle Ages did not merely envy, fear, and hate Lilith. They envied, feared, and *desired* her, too. They used amulets and got "divorces" against the wet dreams she brought them and made their wives wear amulets in childbirth to prevent the death of mother or baby.

In some of the work of feminist writers, femaleness is connected with blood. Women experience menstrual blood as sexy sometimes, at other times as a symbol of their fertility; in any case, very often as energizing. Some men, also, are sexually excited by menstrual blood. Added to this excitement, traditional Jewish men experience the element of forbidden thrill in copulating with a menstrual woman, since traditionally they are not even supposed to touch her. The mingling of this quintessentially female effluent with the male effluent of semen represents a symbiosis that is forbidden to traditional Jews. In the Middle Ages, when the Lilith myth was part of emotional reality, Jewish men shunned the beds of their wives during the menses and for seven days thereafter. They were celibate, therefore, during half their married lives. During these celibate weeks Lilith would appear, to "marry" them in their dreams; her appearance often was connected with blood, namely the menstrual blood of their wives.

Sue D. Burton points to the frequency with which Lilith is identified with "the deep," sometimes also with a bad smell, a stench. In the Kabbalah, she finds Lilith is often described as dressed in "flames from the navel down," or as composed of such flames in her lower regions.

We are reminded of Shakespeare, who says it best, through the lips of Lear:

> Down from the waist they are centaurs
> though women all above
> But to the girdle do the gods inherit.
> Beneath is all the fiends'. There's hell, there's darkness
> There is the sulphurous pit, burning, scalding
> Stench, consumption, fie, fie, fie, pah! Pah! [Act IV, scene 4, 1.124–129]

Like all myths, the myth of Lilith possesses the power to plumb the deepest needs of the human personality. In *Interpretations of Poetry and Religion*, Santayana says that myth and poetry "repair to the material of experience, seizing hold of the reality of sensation and fancy beneath the surface of conventional ideas, and then out of that living but indefinite material . . . build new structures, richer, finer, fitter to the primary tendencies of our nature, truer to the ultimate possibilities of the soul."[1]

The poet mythmaker ". . . dips into the chaos that underlies the rational shell of the world and brings up some superfluous image . . . and reattaches it to the present object . . . If he seems sometimes to obscure a fact, it is only because he is restoring an experience."[2] Who Lilith is, then, depends on the experience of the women who long for her, and upon the needs and fears of the men. Lilith is not afraid of spontaneity—she rides her spontaneity as in the myth she rides the ineffable Name of God. Women long for the courage to exercise their own spontaneity; man may fear spontaneity as a form of loss of self-control; after all, Lilith has control over his desires. So he comes to "diss" spontaneity itself, to disvalue it.

Most of the feminist works reject the threatening, vengeful nature of Lilith in the medieval myth. Why need Lilith take vengeance? She was not deserted in favor of Eve, but left Adam before Eve was created. That he could forget her and be comforted with someone else so soon, perhaps, or that after all there was something enjoyable about her life with Adam, which now someone else enjoys? Where vengeance is suggested, the different works present her as disturbing the peace of the couple by dispatching the snake-tempter (by what power?) or by being the snake herself. As snake-charmer she is the penis-charmer.

One puzzle in the male myth is Lilith's acceptance of the proposed punishment—that she will give birth to one hundred demons every day, which will all die. I suggest that if Lilith is indeed a parent, she takes this as a parent-type threat, the kind she makes herself: "If you eat one more pomegranate before supper, I'll kill you!" Who would believe that God would deliberately kill some of His creatures to punish their mother?

The myth of Lilith expresses the preoccupation of men with the two dangerous powers of women: their power over men's desire, and their power over men's generational continuity: men's preoccupation, that is, with their marital relations—whether in successive or in polygamous marriages. Their need to procreate, with its concomi-

---

1. George Santayana, *Interpretations of Poetry and Religion* (Cambridge, Mass.: Massachusetts Institute of Technology Press, 1989,) p. 161.
2. Ibid., p. 156-57.

tant need for competent and affectionate child care, stands in opposition to their demand that the women beloved of their heart give them her undivided devotion.

In the biblical stories there is often anguish over the fact that the husband of two wives loves one of them much more than the other. The storytellers compensate the less-loved wife with great fertility, which she hopes to use to earn her husband's greater love.

The men want the immortality that children give them, but not at the expense of sharing the love of their favorite woman. So the favorite is often barren! We think of Sarah, Rachel, Hannah (the mother of the prophet Samuel). If she finally does conceive, it is only one child. Rachel has a second one, but his birth kills her. Jacob feels so guilty over this that he prefers her sons to the point of spoiling them. When Sarah finally bears a son to Abraham, he is seized with a compulsion to bring the child as a sacrificial offering. Hannah's son gets to stay with his mother until he is weaned, and then she brings him to the sanctuary and leaves him there forever. Earlier, as she was mumbling a prayer for a child, the priest had accused her of drunkenness. She had expostulated that she is not *that* woman—drunken, sexy—but the maternal one. *Then* she conceived! This story is interesting also for the fact that Hannah's husband expresses his attitude in so many words: "Why fuss because you don't have children? Am I not more to you than ten sons?"

The story of Lilith and Eve is echoed in many ways by the story of Vashti and Esther. The two stories express the same male dream, and a dream dreamed twice, the tradition says, tells truth. The male writer of this tale dreams of his two women: the woman he can't live with, Lilith/Vashti, the wife who is his equal, assured, honest, secure in the dignity of her worth; and Eve/Esther, who rules him through flattery and guile, catering to his vanity and need to feel superior and in charge. We must assume, of course, that although these stories were told as oral literature by women as well as men, they were elaborated by both sexes but written down by men.

They portray the young man as challenged and aroused by a strong, charismatic woman whom he recognizes as an equal. Later, as he ages and tires, the uppity wife is banished, and one who is willing to feign a compliant posture takes her place.

The compliance is feigned, thinly veiling the manipulative natures of Eve and Esther. But this is enough. Her need to bend her nature and become manipulative in itself represents a deep obeisance to his superior power. The man, the woman, and the storyteller all understand that.

She may seem to win through manipulation, but in reality she loses—she must sacrifice her strong, straightforward nature. Lilith, by contrast, choosing to live truthfully and authentically, must banish herself from a marriage in which she is expected to be the subservient partner though she is of equal origin, *ebenbürtig*. Her punishment is a futile fecundity—a withering variation on the theme of love and fertility. Here the Esther/Vashti story seems not to follow suit, for the Lilith figure Vashti disappears from the plot, and no children seem to be mentioned.

But notice this: late in the Esther story, the Lilith character's dark side appears in the person of Zeresh, wife and partner-in-evil of the villain Haman. And her punishment echoes that of Lilith: she has ten sons, and they are all hanged.

The Jewish feminists of the past twenty years take the Lilith myth as their starting point, showing that a revaluation of true value has taken place here. Lilith's good nature—strong, honest, spontaneous—has been demonized and called evil—*das Böse*—while humility, submission, and flattery are praised. Like Nietzsche, they say that this is not good—not *gut*—this humility, being *schlicht*, is actually *schlecht*—rotten. They wish to return to original values, refusing the all-or-nothing, ruler-versus-ruled dichotomy. Some of the works do accept the dichotomy, and in those poems and stories Lilith says no thanks and takes off.

But some of the work points out that this is not the only view of the situation: that there may be love without envy or jealousy, that there may be a possibility of going beyond this-or-that, some new kind of this-and-this-too.

Lilith is still a character-in-progress.

There are family resemblances among the various Lilith characters. A better metaphor perhaps, and even perhaps for family resemblances in general, is that of an old-fashioned kaleidoscope. Variously shaped and colored bits of glass are mirrored so that their tripled and sextupled reflections form a pattern. I turn the tube slightly, there is a slight shift in the bits of glass, so that shapes previously hidden are revealed. Different parts of the totality of glass reflect a completely different pattern—of the same colors—to my eye. A shape changes into another and yet another. Poetic associations draw one another on, keep on transforming in a poetic logic, a pictorial logic, images turning into one another around one element and then around another, which remains stationary for a time.

Then once more I rotate the tube in my hand.

17
The Real First Woman

Rochelle Natt

Skin wan as tallow,
long black hair stripped to a brassy floss,
she appears no more than forty,
though she's the first wife of Adam.
She's taken many names—
Obizuth, Agrat bat Mahalath, Queen of Sheba...

Now she calls herself Lola
and lives in a small apartment in Brooklyn.
She loves it when the train clatters by on the El,
blocking out the light,
so like her cave...
All her children have flown to California
where they practice the Black Arts.
How proud she is that they've only killed outsiders
unlike Adam and Eve's two.

What a relief it was to flee from Eden—
that endless green and those insipid rivers
and Adam trying to lord it over her.
Even Eve, that fawning bitch,
had the sense to bite temptation.

Late at night, Lola slips into bed with pious old men.
She has grown fonder of them than demons.
Hairless, toothless, soft-fleshed,
they give up their God
and pension checks
to nibble on her breasts.

18
Riding the Wind's Wing

Ruth Feldman

Half of me is beautiful
but you were never sure
which half. You lay with me
of your own free will, then fled
back to her chaste bed.
The mother of your real children

hangs an amulet with magic syllables
over their cribs,
to ward me off.

Sitting beside her
on the Sabbath bench, you
exorcise me. I come back, riding

the wind's wing, slip through
the walls and steal into bed
between you. You wake spent.

Each time your loins
twitch with desire,
my womb swells with a new burden.

Our children multiply like seeds.
They will wail at your deathbed
and crowd her children out. But not

for long. Robbed of their birthright,
my frail progeny will fade and die
as her brood grows rosier.[1]

---

1. One of the many legends that have grown up around Lilith is that every time a man has relations with a woman in his mind or in a dream, he fathers a child upon this female demon. These children are frail, sickly, and short-lived.

19

Lilith's Daughters

Frieda Singer

[Lilith] responded, "We are both equal because we both come from the earth."
—*Alphabet of Ben Sira 23a–b*

"And God created the human species... man and woman created He them"
—*Genesis: 1:27*

My father is massaging my back.
I am ten; his fingers move like scissors
through my hair before pressing upon
vertebrae along the spine, and my father
holding the evening paper while I solve
equations on the porcelain-topped
kitchen table, the coffee already cold,
the cat arching his back
along the sides of our legs.

Fingers fan outward
to wings of shoulder blade
and collar bone:
sweet plums of touch.

More tentatively, my husband rubs
my back today as if he were not yet
accustomed to how skin grips bone,
how it flows into inlets,
nestles in mounds.

We are only a few years into that place
where women leave children while they work,
where women, also, ask of their men at night
a smoothing out even as harbors

tides have assaulted, contrive, finally,
a hollowing into gullies and coves.
So, I am patient, stroke his chest,
wait until he becomes more and more
like the wind outside, buffing
the leaves, pummeling the spine
of the evergreen,
and, as gentle.

20

Divine Mornings

Susan Gold

He once let her breathe deep
into an ear of his apple orchard,
and she could feel his sky's chest sigh.

Lilith knows where God's eyes can be found;
she has kissed them.

And when she wakes
to find the earth's sheets wet with dew,
she knows he still dreams of her.

21
Surrounded by Satyrs, Lilith Takes a Stand

Elaine Frankonis

Suddenly, they are all around me,
  their jagged tracks
  pointing in all directions,
etched into the earth like runes,
battered circles, omens of confusion.

They speak without words—
a slow lidding of eyes,
curving of mouth, writhing of tongue.
Their dappled shadows prance
to an overture of leaves,
a crescendo of sun.

My body begins to dance in answer,
smell their musk,
taste their salty stream,
sense their strokes of fine hairs,
coarse skin, and
(yes, yes . . .)

Until the cloud, the cold—
a cold of mind,
an absence of heart.

I force myself to speak,
and the words break the spell,
their magic stronger
than even that basest call:

And then what, my friends,
what then, when it is over,
and the night wind finds our skin,
urging us to a place safe for dreaming?
What then, when morning steals our union,
and you scamper away,
hungry for the day's diversions—
impromptu symphonies of senses?

And, worse still,
what if you stay,
and I am caught in your silent
single-minded worship
of a world without words?

I have been here before, my friends,
have reached into that dark fire
blazing so far from the hearth—
that ancient seething
that (even now)
I breathe from you,
feed from you,
send to my nightly cauldron
to simmer and stir
to ladle, at last,
into mounds of midnight words,
this witch's brew.

In the failing light,
the satyrs shift
and snort their disaffections;
their shadows sink into stones
too high for holding.

I leave those stones to claim
their wordless dreams.

22
Lilith Returns

Elaine Frankonis

And it came to pass that Adam and Eve stayed in Eden. And where they stepped, the sky rolled along an even noon blue, and shadows never found their eyes for there was no hiding. All paths were marked, neat and visible and orderly, and for many days, Adam was happy, knowing the lay of his land, the petals of every flower, the leaves of every tree; knowing the end of every journey and the edge of every limit.

And Eve saw her place, knew the way the wind blew, and turned her back accordingly.

And so it went, until after a while, God sensed that Eve was growing a little restless and Adam was growing a little bored (and even he himself—although he never would admit it—began to seek a little diversion).

And so he went to Adam and said, "Look, fella, have I got a deal for you. If you go over near the Northern boundaries of Eden and eat some fruit from a certain tree—which I will tell you about in a minute—it will make your life here a little more interesting. It's called the Tree of Reason, and I think it will be very much to your liking. Not only is it tasty, but you can amuse yourself for hours inventing games with its seeds. Which, by the way, are shaped like question marks . . ."

And then he went to Eve and said, "Hiya, cutie. Look, I thought you might like to know that I have an interesting tree growing near the Southern boundary of Eden. Why don't you go over there and try some of its fruit? It is absolutely delicious. Its seeds are shaped like little exclamation points, and you can amuse yourself playing with them for hours. It's called the Tree of Intuition..."

And so, both being obedient children, Adam and Eve did as God suggested and never wondered at the wisdom of it all, and never thought to exchange information or ask God what the hell he was up to.

And so it came to pass that, indeed, Adam and Eve found the trees that God had promised. Each ate of the fruit of the assigned tree, and each came to know the pleasure of its seeds. They found the fruit very much to their liking, indeed—so much so, that Adam spent more and more of his time in the North, and Eve spent more and more of her time in the South.

And on those rare occasions when they would find themselves in the same place at the same time, it seemed that they no longer could understand each other's language, each other's gestures. And so they spent more and more time in their own places, with their own visions, and with their own seeds.

And while Adam and Eve buried the seeds of their dreams in different parts of Eden, there was another yet who lived and dreamed in what was called The Rest of the World. She was Lilith, Adam's first wife, who some say was driven out of, and who some say chose to leave, the sameness and safety of Eden to search for the magical Tree of Knowledge that was said to grow somewhere out in The Rest of the World.

But as much as she searched The Rest of the World, Lilith was never able to find that one Tree of Knowledge. She did, however, eat regularly of the fruits of the Tree of Reason and the Tree of Intuition—and also of the Tree of Sensation and the berries of any number of tangled vines, such as Curiosity and Mistakes and Risk and Love and Joy and Pain. Sometimes she ate so much she thought she would burst with it all. And sometimes no matter how much she ate, she was still hungry, and so she knew that the hunger had nothing to do with eating.

While Lilith came to love The Rest of the World, it was not the easy place that was Eden. Lilith had to learn a lifetime of survival skills, and many of these she learned from an assortment of friends who also had chosen to leave Eden for more challenging arenas. She came to know them as Possum and Fox, Bear and Salamander, and most certainly Osprey, who joined with her as a knowing guide and a fierce friend. Some shared with her their hides and furs to make a protective covering for herself; some shared their gifts of sight and flight. They taught her when to flow and when to strike, when to become earth and when to become air.

And it came to pass that Adam, who for some reason was very fond of sunsets, took to spending more and more of his time traveling between the Northern and the Western parts of Eden, taking the fruits of his Reason to enjoy as he lay on the ever-soft grasses of Eden's Western shores. There he filled himself and rested and wondered at the intriguing sounds drifting over from The Rest of the World—the cries, the babbles, the moans, the laughter. And he heard them as the music that they were—the music of creatures who lived among the tangled vines and fruitful trees, among the surprising thunder and fire and stones of The Rest of the World.

And it came to pass in time that Lilith's hunger took her along the Western borders of Eden, where one evening she saw Adam from across the long road between them. From the safety of the shadows that veiled The Rest of the World, she watched Adam, watching. And in time Lilith found that she was able to name the hunger she felt even when full of the fruit and berries and roots and nuts and even the seeds of The Rest of the World.

And so, she watched, and waited, and danced with the shadows and sang with the Oak for longer than she could remember, until one unusually bright evening when the moon shone full on the edges of Eden, she straightened her hides, brushed her hair, nibbled on a few nuts of Courage, took a deep breath, and strode up to the boundary between Eden and The Rest of the World.

"Adam," Lilith called, and Adam felt a forgotten stirring deep inside himself, a stirring that caused his eyes to open a little more and his grip on Reason to slip—almost.

"Come with me," Lilith sang. "Wander with me through these sweet and tangled vines that hold my home in The Rest of the World, and I will seed you a feast for your heart's bursting."

"You've got to be kidding. It's a madhouse out there," Adam replied, swallowing the stirring deep within him and washing it down with a bite of his filling fruit. "And anyway, it is Eve I want."

"Do you now!" sneered Lilith, remembering the first rebuke and retrieving her discarded hides. "And when is the last time you really saw Eve, anyway? When is the last time you cared to look for her, look at her with your eyes wide open?

"While you were sitting here wondering at the sounds drifting in from The Rest of the World and munching on your limited diet, what do you suppose happened to Eve? I'll tell you what happened. She has hidden herself in a perfect grove deep in the heart of Eden. Her dragon guards the boundaries of her life in the grove, and as she waits now for a perfect hero to rescue her, she prays that in his battle for her own perfection, he does not trample her tidy garden and ruin her perfect roses, and if he does, she hopes the dragon will dispose of him, neatly, of course."

Adam rose from his ease on Eden's earth. "Maybe so," replied Adam, looking down at Lilith who even in her armor seemed to be dwarfed by Adam, so filled with the fruits of his Reason. "But maybe not," he continued. "That is only your interpretation.

"Reason tells me that I know better what the truth is. And the truth is that Eden is the way it's supposed to be, a place where the boundaries have been set, a place where what I want is within reach, a place where I have counted the petals of each flower and know each one by name. A place where each path is marked and I always know where I am."

Slowly, Lilith moved farther out from the shadows that followed her from The Rest of the World. She walked closer to the shifting boundary between their worlds and removed the hides from her head and her chest and her arms.

She stood before him, wings and talons, mosses and honey; she smelled of wild herbs crushed on the forest floor.

"Adam," she whispered to his eyes, hidden under her shadow. "We are both tired of being alone. I have been hiding in the wild of The Rest of the World and you are hiding in an Eden not of your creation.

"I have watched you watching the sun endlessly slip behind the fiery Western horizon, listening to music that touches you but you cannot touch. Come with me and I will show you the other side of the mountain, where the sun smolders through all the nights; I will take you to the music maker that is your shadow, the teacher who will give you eyes to see in the dark.

"Your shadow has wings, Adam. It dances and sings and waits outside of Eden."

And Adam opened his eyes and cried.

23
Lilith Healing and Aging

Lilly Rivlin

In the uncertain ebb and flow of time and emotions, much of one's life history is etched in the senses. And things of no particular importance, or irreplaceable things, can suddenly resurface in a cafe one winter's night.
—Banana Yoshimoto, Kitchen

"**G**o home, Go home to the desert," the voice within urged. And Leah listened.

I knew I had to get home like a salmon knows it has to get back to its spawning ground. Over eons of time I have wandered the world, often a participant, sometimes an observer, of the human condition. I remember Eden almost as a dream. My memory is filled with patches of forgetfulness. I continue to love and embrace the Other, momentarily merging, but always returning to a differentiated self. An image of a snake with its tail in its mouth, an Uroboros, is indelibly etched in my mind. It is my inner compass to reach home.

Her entire journey was instinctual. Only in Israel did Leah realize she had to return to the shores of the Red Sea. When her cousin asked why she had come, she didn't mention Lilith. She said, "*nikui rosh*," which means to clean your head.

Imagine *falling in love at sixty*. For the last three months Leah had been in turmoil and despair. It happened last summer, in her sixtieth year after she had finally accepted her fate: she was destined to spend the rest of her life alone. When an invitation arrived to present her work at a film festival in Colorado, she was delighted. She stepped through a white wooden gate leading to the garden reception for the filmmakers, a contented woman who knew where she had come from and where she was going.

"Ah, a Spanish gentleman," she thought as she spotted him immediately in the throng. A haughty bearing with hair pulled back in a short, stubby ponytail and a well-trimmed dark beard, he was the only man among the laid-back crowd dressed in an Armani jacket. This was his coming-out party, his first baby steps in the dating game. She hadn't known it then.

Near the swimming pool talking to another female filmmaker, she felt someone's eyes on her. "Leah?" She glanced up to the Spanish gentlemen looking at her with affection. "Seth Marx." A familiar name but she couldn't place him. "Anthropology 101." Thirty-five years ago they had been in a class together. They started talking. He had married, had three children, opened up a factory and made a fortune, and had recently liquidated his business. He had just divorced. He was intense. Now she remembered thirty-five years ago, he had stood before her after class talking and she had floated away from him to protect herself from that very intensity.

She invited him to a party she was giving that afternoon. When he walked in, she was pleasantly surprised. She circulated among her guests but felt drawn to this man who was a stranger yet whom she had known for her entire life. Later, as she walked him to the door, she said, "I'm looking for a partner, I'm looking for my equal." The words had tumbled out of her mouth. Two days later she called him. They met on Friday and went to bed that night. He could not have an orgasm but he pleasured her greatly. In return, he wanted her to give him physical pain. Though she had known, in the biblical sense, numerous men, she had never had such a request and found it difficult to comply. On Monday she flew back to New York City. Upon her return she found a tender message from him on her machine. For the next few weeks they spoke almost daily, like teenagers, smitten by passion. They made preparations to meet, this time on her turf.

She took a risk and jumped in and found herself warmly embraced, with lavish gifts and deep intimacies. To love passionately once more was all that mattered! It was a whirlwind romance. He took her to Paris for her sixtieth birthday, they stayed at the Ritz, and for the next six weeks they were inseparable, traveling to England, Italy, Czechoslovakia, Hungary, Turkey, and Israel, painting pictures of longer future stays in favorite places. They went to museums, visited antiquities, made love, had a major argument, flew over

Jerusalem and Masada in a four-seater plane, and parted at Heathrow, already having planned their next meeting.

At the end he spoke her words, the words that she had always left others with, "I want my space and freedom." Her words from his mouth. Her body shook; she could not stop heaving—dry heaves that left her spent and empty. After his departure he sent her Mary Oliver's latest book of poems with a bookmark in the page where "The Journey" appeared.

She knew that poem well; she had read it to him on New Year's Eve in Costa Rica. It described a solitary journey. It spoke of the need to save in "the only life you could save": your own.

His message was clear. Though she understood his need for freedom, she felt banished from his life.

Some say I was banished from Eden, others claim my speaking God's name aloud caused my expulsion, but I left of my own free will. I had to leave in order to breathe, I had to leave in order to live.

At the Egyptian border the drivers wait for passengers to fill their dilapidated taxis for the run to Sharm-el-Sheikh. The familiar voice whispered, "Lilith returns to the Red Sea." Leah looked to see if anyone else heard it, but the drivers, reclining on the wooden benches, continued to brush away flies, undisturbed by the passing of time. One by one travelers, sun-browned bodies decorated with tattoos, arrived with backpacks and haggled with the drivers over the fare while she watched and remembered that she was one of them thirty years ago.

She went to the Red Sea in the Sinai desert to heal herself. A friend from Jerusalem had told her about La Calmata, a quiet cluster of whitewashed stone houses along a beautiful sandy beach on the Red Sea. Outside the room was a small terrace about seventy-five feet from the beach. Inside the shades were drawn to keep the sun out. The room had two single beds with wafer-like mattresses on wooden bases, a simple closet, a small refrigerator, and, to her joy and delight, a sparkling white-tiled bathroom with a stall shower. She had thought to stay nearby at the Bedouin encampment, which also had stone houses, but the prospect of going outside in the middle of the night for the inevitable pee put her off.

Now she is home by the Red Sea. Golden glowing clouds are suspended above her head, behind, the mauve mountains, in front, the continuation of the Aqaba mountain range which runs through Jordan and Saudi Arabia. Stillness enters her soul. She wants to cry from joy.

Each time I return to the Red Sea I am filled with joy. The men have written of my orgies with centaurs, Minotaurs and demons; the truth is far from that, the truth is I have created a space of stillness, of pure energy and sensual delight where the art of dreaming can be practiced to return the energy flow to the universe. Yes, it is also a space for sexual and sensual delight, but those who have maligned my name in the name of Order and God, refuse to acknowledge the Body and Spirit connection. They fear their lack of inner balance.

"I am sixty," Leah thought, observing it from within and without, while stroking her still youthful lean body, as she masturbated with the small but powerful sleek dildo Seth had given her. At the border, a young Egyptian convinced her to take a taxi to the "station." He didn't want her to stay in the sun because of her fair skin, he said. "This sun is not for old people." She was stunned to be regarded as an old person. She had to remind herself that she was sixty. She was equally stunned to find out that the "station" was only two city blocks away. On the way to La Calmata, she had passed the castle that Saladin built when he conquered Egypt; she remembered being there thirty years before with Mario, the great love of her life, the man she had left her husband for. She had an orgasm and was grateful to be alive.

When she awoke from a deep sleep, the sun was setting. Languishing on the bed, she stretched her long legs like a cat, her thoughts inexorably returning to Seth. Once more she went over their last trip together to Costa Rica at the end of December. She thought they were having a wonderful time. A month later, he told her he had been thinking of his ex-wife on New Year's Eve, yet on Valentine's Day he sent a dozen red roses with a card: "I wish I was with you today. I remember our wonderful New Year's Eve in Costa Rica . . ."

After a brief shower she walked to the beach, which was covered with small round rocks whose smooth surfaces soothed the soles of her feet. Wading into the clear shallow water she remembered lying on the beach in Costa Rica watching Seth, oar in hand, push a yellow raft out into the blue lagoon. He smiled, waving to her like a little boy eagerly setting out for his first adventure. She was filled with love for him and unable to fathom his departure.

After sunset, she made her way to a table in front of a large Bedouin tent where dinner was being served. A few stars were already visible. There was only one other guest, a slim young woman who also sat alone reading by the light of a candle embedded in sand in a plastic container. The candles took her back fourteen years, the last time she had been in the Sinai, then under Israeli rule, for a gathering of Jews, Muslims, Sufis, and Christians who had come together to talk about peace. Now she was back in Sinai, this time under Egyptian rule. Then she was trying to make peace between Arabs and Jews, now she was searching for peace within.

"A beautiful moon tonight," she says to the handsome young headwaiter hovering around her. "It's almost full," he replies, as he lights her cigarette, "like you."

After dinner, she retired to her terrace. A soft white mist covered the night sky. She gazed at the stars waiting for a message from the moon.

That night she had erotic dreams of centaurs and Minotaurs, harking back to Mario, whose erotic imagination was a cornucopia of mythical animals. When she woke up she remembered her horoscope: Don't give in to your sexual appetite. Her therapist had echoed that very same injunction. "You went to bed with Seth immediately; next time get to know the guy first, maybe you'll spot the dysfunctionality earlier."

In the morning she is on the beach inspecting the thousands of embryonic jellyfish washed ashore. Nearby thousands more float on the water's surface like a jeweled quilted blanket, waiting their turn to be washed ashore. Once she was a sun worshiper; now she wears a hat and applies sun lotion as she settles down to read a script and ready herself for healing. Throughout the morning Ibrahim, the barman, comes by to take her order. Like the headwaiter, he has a mustache, dark eyes, olive skin, and a strong presence. Unabashedly he surveys her body and she, attracted by the directness of the exchange, returns the gaze. He offers to teach her backgammon in the afternoon. But after lunch the Chamsin, a strong warm wind from the North, blows the thatched palm shelters on the beach, stirring the sand, whirling it around, transforming it from soft granules to abrasive and gritty bits. Welcoming the storm, she takes pleasure in the sharp stings of the swirling sand, which pierce her skin like thin needles. When it becomes painful, she retreats to her room. Soon she is fast asleep.

When I left Eden in the North and came South to the Red Sea I caused the sand to swirl and whirl, and it was called Chamsin. Often I sat on the shore, the waves licking at my feet, while the Chamsin enfolded me in an embrace that reminded me of the hot breath of the lover I had on the Aegean Sea on my way from Eden . . .

She returns at dusk. The tide has turned, small fluffy waves lick the shore. Ibrahim brings her water.

"Why you not go in?"

"Because of the jellyfish," she answers. She had waded in earlier but was put off by the presence of the gelatinous white blobs with their purple centers oozing sexuality.

"The Red Sea is full of jellyfish. They come out when it is cloudy, otherwise they stay beyond the corals," he tells her.

Baby jellyfish multiply like my children. In the story that men tell about me, when I refused to go back to Adam, God caused one hundred of my children to perish daily. I know I have to go into the depths of the Red Sea to search for them.

He offers her a joint, which she declines for now, but promises to return that evening for backgammon. Curious, she asks him where La Calmata's water supply comes from. "For cooking is desalinized water from the station, for showers is water from the mountains, for drinking is Baarakat in bottle," he replies. They are interrupted by the headwaiter who strides over as if on a mission. He says something to Ibrahim in Arabic. Leah senses that the men are vying for her attention. She wonders if they have any idea of her age. The small waves lapping at the shore have almost ceased.

Though she is afraid, Leah arranges to rent snorkeling equipment. She has a tightness in her belly, her breath is irregular as she walks to the coral reef, quite far from the shore, telling herself: Don't panic. Breathe in and out, like in a meditation.

The instructor, a bronzed and toned German, refuses to let her go alone when he learns she has not snorkeled for thirty years. Unlike the other men at La Calmata, he shows no interest in her as a woman. He is taciturn and correct. "When we get there pull the snorkel over your nose and follow me," he instructs carefully. "It's a sudden drop, like jumping off the top of a mountain. I'll be with you all the time. Don't panic!" He lowers the snorkel over his mouth and motions her to follow. She jumps in after him.

Home again. I enter another time zone inhabited by sea urchins, a rainbow of fish observe me from bulging eyes. A barber fish swims by, resplendent in its multicolored scales. Above me a shadow appears—thou-

sands of embryonic jellyfish form an opaque umbrella overhead. I recognize them. They are my children. I am a childless woman and these are my Lilim. I move to embrace them. They engulf me.

I remember Adam. I will always love Adam, I have looked into his soul. That is why he ran to God—he was so frightened. I have also looked into God's soul within me. I can't breathe now. I force my arms through the Lilim and burst forth for air.

Leah remembers visiting this shimmering sea-green world with Mario; she remembers a childhood story of Curdie, the chimney sweep swimming under the sea. In her peripheral vision she sees the instructor motioning her to get away from the baby jellyfish. She stretches her arms up to touch them. He dives below and pushes her up through the surface of the sea, pulling her to the reef where she can stand. "I'm fine," she tells him as she walks toward shore.

Ibrahim stands on shore. "You O.K.?" he asks handing her a towel. "I'm fine," she assures him dropping into a chair. He gives her water. "You come to bar and we play backgammon." She nods her head, tired but exhilarated. Very patiently he teaches her the game. She wins twice and knows he is letting her. They talk about how one knows one's path. Coming to the Sinai was following his path. Both of them are aware that he must attend to the other guests who have come into the bar area. Not wanting his attention to be noticed by the manager, she gets up to leave. "You come tonight," he says. She is struck by his clarity and confidence. They arrange to meet after the bar closes.

In her room she tells herself not to give in to her sexual appetite. She resolves not to sleep with him. After showering with water from the mountains, she applies lotion over her body, lies on the bed, and brings herself to orgasm, mindful of her self-sufficiency thanks to Seth's gift. He was full of fear like Adam, she thinks, without pain.

When the bar closed and all the lights were off, she walked on the beach with Ibrahim. He held her hand. They smoked a joint. He told her about his girlfriend of six years whom he had planned to marry until one day she told him she was marrying another man. "It broke my heart," he said. "Mine is broken, too," she confides. He touches her breast. He is handsome and virile and though flattered that he desires her, she moves his hand away, believing this will impede her journey. She wants to be bathed by the rays of the moon. She wants energy and wisdom from the moon. Gently but firmly, she explains this to him. Though he says he understands English, she doubts he understands all she has said. "The moon grows larger," he says. "Tomorrow it will be full."

The next day she ventures beyond La Calmata to the Bedouin encampment where the "travelers" stay. On her walk she passes the Sinai Moon, a palm-covered spacious restaurant of limited selection, which looks like a Bedouin tent with discrete reclining areas of colorful Bedouin pillows and rugs around low center tables. Another mustachioed man in his early thirties with beautiful dark eyes beckons to her from the entrance. "I give you coffee, you teach me new English words," he says. She promises to come back for two bottles of Baarakat water as they are half the price La Calmata charges. On her return Lutfi introduces himself, practicing his broken English. A charmer in his early thirties, Lutfi spent his twenties shuttling among Libya, Egypt, and Syria smuggling gold; now, *ein shala* (God willing), he can relax. He offers Leah a joint. He too is a moon worshiper. "The moon is full tonight," he raises his eyebrows appealingly. A soft breeze wafts through the tent, enveloping them. She relaxes back into the pillows while in the background John Denver sings *Sweet Surrender*. Lutfi winks at her. She feels a desirable woman.

She walks back to La Calmata talking to the moon. She thinks of Seth calmly. If it is meant to be it will be, she muses as she sits on a bar stool watching Ibrahim serve drinks. Nothing is accidental, she thinks, as once again she tunes into the words of the tape in the background, *"I've got to let you go, no more sleepless nights."* Ibrahim looks at her as he mixes a drink. He wants to meet again. "But it will be like last night, you understand." "I understand," he says. She hopes he really does. Not that he is undesirable but she wants to remain in herself. She is healing.

They walked again on a path along the shore. This time he was insistent. In the middle of the path, he quickly pulled her silk trousers down, but her underwear, entangled with her trousers, slowed him down, giving her time to explain there would be no pleasure for either of them if it would be against her will. "Why you wear underwear?" he asked. Apparently other women he had been with had not. She always wore underwear. A certain intimacy had been established between them. They agreed to sit at a nearby sand dune to contemplate the moon. She wanted him to know about her inner Lilith voice and why she had come to La Calmata. But he couldn't understand. Impatiently, he reached for her hand; she responded. He kissed her. He whispered, "Moon is for man woman make love." Soon he was on top of her; she pulled her trousers and underwear down. When he penetrated far beyond anyone else's reach she stopped the story in her head and surrendered to the waves sweeping through her *kus*.

She made love to Ibrahim in the full moonlight. He was like a centaur, his bold penis illuminated by the moon. At first she resisted, fearful of her sexual appetite and then she heard the voice: *Lilith, become who you are.* She surrendered. She mounted him. It was not a meeting of souls but it quenched the flames of her passion.

The waves continued as she pulled up her underwear and silk pants and during their walk back along the beach and even in the welcoming hot shower she took back at La Calmata.

The next day, her last in the desert, she woke up renewed. The days had passed without awareness of time. She sat in her beach chair noting the arrival of Israeli families with children, their voices filling the air. Nearby a herd of goats grazed. Ibrahim passed by several times carrying drinks to the new guests. He was cool; only flashes of a grin acknowledged their shared secret. No mythologies, it is only moment to moment, she thinks, as she resolved not to join him on the beach that night in spite of the moon.

In the late afternoon she walked to the Sinai Moon to share a last joint with Lutfi. This time, Jacobo, a tall thin black man in a *galabiya*, with a Walkman on his ears, joins them. Leah assumed he was a Bedouin. "*Ja* people," he says leaning over for a light. "What do you mean?" "*Ja* means Jewish in Jamaican, he said, putting the earphones to her ear to hear Bob Marley sing about the Exodus, slavery, and liberation. Recently graduated from the University of Cairo, he was from the Sudan, a country rich in resources but prevented from developing by neighbors who prefer to keep it as a source of cheap labor. But, he tells her, the next generation is different.

Her talks in Israel with friends and family had left her despondent about future prospects for peace but hearing Jacobo gave her hope. Yet, a cautionary interior voice warned, we all know that people-to-people contact does not prevent wars. Karl Deutsch, a renowned political scientist, measured the communication patterns between Germans and French immediately before the outbreak of

World War I, and found them to be at their zenith. This is peace, she insisted, this is what she had hoped for. "Do you know about the New Age, Global Earth, humanism . . ." she asks Jacobo. He lights up with recognition. "*The Celestine Prophecy, The Tenth Insight*, I read them both. Now I am reading the third book. Everyone reads it here." This is Global Earth, she thinks sinking further back into the pillows. A soft wind passes through the Sinai Moon. Bliss.

"Were you always so . . . so," she searched for the right word, "evolved?" He grins. "After I graduated I came to the Sinai, all the prophets were here. From the Sinai came the Spirit, *Ruach, Ruchi*. I listened to the wind and watched the stillness. I asked myself why I have to accept my parents' religion just because I grew up in their home." Clearing his mind of prior beliefs, he began building layer upon layer of an identity based on the new concepts. Maybe there will be a new spirit in the world, she thought.

I remembered the Throbbing Spirit whirling in the Chaos, I remembered the pulse of the Universe. In that space I and Thou encountered and Energy was born. And there came a new generation that knew how to listen to the Wind and to the Stillness and to contemplate Nothingness. And this generation brought forth from its Center the knowledge of the Life Force and that the Holy Energy is in each and every one of us.

Amal, Amal, she said using the Arabic word for hope that Lutfi had taught her. "I hope, too," Jacobo says. A soft wind like a giant genie's breath embraced them. They watched the full moon low on the horizon as it began its ascent. Jacobo broke the silence. "The moon and the sea are intertwined. Until midnight it will be calm and then the wind will change. I think that is a scientific fact," he said looking to Leah for confirmation. "The moon and the earth go around the sun, yes?" "Yes," she said, "it is a scientific fact." She turned to Lutfi, so hungry for knowledge that his eyes glazed from listening to a conversation he longed to understand. "Jacobo can teach you English—and more. You understand?" "No," he laughed. "Jacobo, *targem lo*," she said. Jacobo translated. Lutfi smiled broadly. "I understand." Jacobo rose, bid farewell, and walked to the beach to commune with the moon.

Leah returned to La Calmata. It was her last night by the Red Sea. She sat at the beach savoring each moment as she gazed at the moon waiting for a message. Ibrahim appeared. "Come in ten minutes. I want to talk to you." "Fifteen," she said. An image of she and Seth dancing on the beach at midnight on New Year's Eve came to her mind. She forced herself to watch it float by. It's an old program, she thought, knowing he would always be in her heart. The voice echoed within: *The message is within you.* She walked to the bar. "What did you want to tell me," she asked. "Don't wear underwear. I have condoms," he said. "My *kus* was full of sand last night." "You wash it," he replies, matter-of-fact. "Sometimes it is best to have a one-time experience and remember it forever," she tells him. They play their last game of backgammon and he wins. At midnight she goes to her room to sleep until Ibrahim closes the bar.

She wakes up to discover it is after 2 a.m. Had she slept through his phone call? She goes to the terrace. There are no lights in the bar. What happened? Perhaps the phone didn't work. Maybe he got scared or fell asleep. Still digesting the message—it is all within you— she goes out to look at the moon for the last time. Perhaps he went with his friends to Dahab. What am I getting out of this? she asks herself. Delicious anticipation. In expectation of making love in the moonlight, she feels her *kus* pulsate like a flower opening and closing. Had she given him double signals? Is this a lesson, she wonders? And if so, what is to be learned? That some things cannot be changed. One can, however, seek an explanation. Will he offer an explanation? Perhaps there will be no explanation. Was Seth's desire for space and freedom an explanation? "It is all in the realm of trust," said the voice, "trust yourself and then you can trust others." Ibrahim and I have trust between us, she thinks.

Stroking her nipples, she opens *When Nietzsche Wept*, the book she has been reading all along on the trip, and reads the next passage: "If you choose to be one of those few who partake of the pleasure of growth and the exhilaration of godless freedom, then you must prepare yourself for the greatest pain . . ." She knows nothing is accidental. "The spirit of man is constructed out of his choices." When she was young she knew this; now it was time to reclaim it. She falls asleep comfortable with these thoughts. On the verge of dropping off into a deep sleep, the phone rings. It's Ibrahim. "I'm not going out," she tells him angrily.

"I have to talk to you."

"Where were you?"

"I want to tell you what happened."

An explanation. She dresses; she does not put on underwear.

What happened? He saw her as she walked to the bar but he was unable to call to her because he was with the manager and owner in the Bedouin tent under darkness still on duty. By now she knew he was a proud man; she knew he needed his job. They walk. He tells her about his two-hour search that afternoon for a condom. The pharmacy was closed during the siesta break, and though he was on duty, he went to a Bedouin friend who had only two condoms, one for his own use that night, and one he gave to Ibrahim. Amused and appreciative of his effort she is aware that his absence, if discovered, would have jeopardized his job. He kisses her, breathing smoke into her. They caress each other; she feels his tight muscular body pressing into her. Aroused, he takes out his phallus, which glistens in the full light of the moon. He wants to enter her immediately. "Trust me," she tells him taking his hand as she leads him to a sand dune nearby, which offers the comfort of a curved incline to recline against. With his erect manhood uncomfortably between his legs he follows the object of his desire. *Shwayeh, shwayeh*, slowly, slowly, she tells him as he pulls the condom over his shiny and swollen penis, which reminds her of Brancusi's *Bird in Flight*.

Bathed by the rays of the moon he entered my kus *that has been throbbing and waiting to receive him since yesterday. I let him mount me and it was good. I felt an electric current charge through my body like a bolt of lightning, and I was full of the cosmic Energy. And the spirit in me was called the Life Force. And it was good.*

Only in this way could she stop thinking. This exchange of energy between man and woman was the connecting Life Force. Nothing was accidental. She is carried away on an oceanic wave as a light wind caresses their naked sex. In the deep recesses of her mind she is aware of Seth in the breeze, like a strand that will always be with her, joining the other loves of her life as she continues her own journey.

There under the gaze of the Moon, Leah resolved to get a small tattoo of the Uroboros above her *kus* when she returned to New York City.

III
LILITH AS TRANSGRESSIVE WOMAN

For centuries men created Midrash, legends, even songs, depicting Lilith as a transgressive woman. Now, probably for the first time in history, women write about Lilith—as an alluring and destructive, unredeemed and outrageous dark being—from their point of view.

In the following three poems and short story she emerges as a timeless demon—a devouring witch torched by flames, a Russian lover/mistress who reappears as Cousin Izzy's first wife, an American slut; and as a vampire-like figure transmuting from woman to Chameleon. In a punk-inspired short story Lilith is all-powerful and evil; she is the devil incarnate.

As women have recovered Lilith and made her their own, we note the brevity of this chapter compared to the others. It would appear that contemporary women have chosen to incorporate the transgressive nature of Lilith into a fuller, more textured representation.

24

The First Woman

Ruth Whitman

Those limbs were never fashioned for a human:
too small, too fine, too delicate for the eye.

Her brittle wrist, her childlike hands and feet
confuse the mind, mix pity with desire.

She smiles to bite, she kisses to devour!
The opal of delight, the lusting stars,

the concupiscent grass, the whole world moves
in eager love beneath her naked feet

We caught the witch and bound her bruised and bare,
crushed back the smiles and kisses in her blood,

and flung our faggots on her luminous hair.

25
For the Lilith Archives

Mindy Rinkewich

Archetype of aliases
unhallowed extra
the one who wasn't supposed to be there
but there she was
fifth wheel for the wagon, my pious grandmas called her.
Lyubovnitsa, my tight-lipped grandmas called her,
Russian for lover, mistress, only more so.
Implied contempt and eroticism enforced by system.
Prissy poverty of Tsarist Russia:
spotless homes, spotless morals,
their only claim to status.

Ah, Lyubovnitsa, taking shape
from the steam and talk over their tea glasses,
exuding a delicious sinfulness
my American Lilly could never hope to equal.
Only the innocence of their forgotten corner
could stimulate such imaginings.
Bubbi. I prefer my instant coffee
To your trite tea any day.
I'll match your fifth wagon wheel with my spare tire,
and I'll add a safety valve
with a dash of sophistication beyond your possibilities
as I am beyond
The pots and prayer books of your border town.

We're talking about two different people.
I see the summer slut,
I take in the sounds beneath the boardwalk.
To you she is the icy gust
coming through a crack in your January window
in a land where the snow is blue as my skies.
She dances over the blue on bare feet white as my snows,
the sweet fadeout of the lost traveler
dying on blue bed linen
while his wife waits outside the house,
gloved hand swinging a lantern in the night.

She shows up—sooner or later—inevitably
on a Workmen's Circle membership list
sparking a stack of dissertations
as to whether they ganged up on her
and drove her from their winter wonderland
All stomping boots and frostbitten self-righteousness.
She came running westward after them
when they had had it with the blood and ice,
the place—no place for nice Jewish girls,
not even for those who weren't so nice
not even for those who weren't Jewish.
It never really was for real
the sandcastle beneath those rustling pines.

She makes it big here,
muse of sillysongsingers,
allowed, at last, to tell it all—
America is their poetic license.

Sweet land of just come out and say
any damn thing that happens to pop
into your fool head.
shameless serenaders of
summer slut
swimming pool siren
Catskill cutie
of our young Julys and Augusts
they got or didn't get,
I, sulking along sidepaths,
snotty, sometimes idealistic,
touch of the grandmas

watching them worship Golden Girl,
worshiping Golden Calf in Golden Land,
admit knowing her personally.

All right, Lilly,
Cousin Izzy's first wife,
stealer of handsome kissing cousins.
Didn't love him
"I just wanted to see if I could get him."

So she throws a fox jacket over her g-string,
steps into her open-toe open-back pumps
(that was dressing up)
goes out and gets him
trying to see if she can get him
into a wartime marriage.
Two-timed him while he was in Italy getting shot,
triple-timed him after he came marching home
and started working his butt off for her.
Looking back fifty years
from vantage points of America of the nineties,
two-out-of-three marriages on the rocks,
And they know it when they're first starting out.
Big deal—Lilly!

26
Chameleon
F. Dianne Harris

Under the new moon,
　　Lilith sambas
　　her cloven-hooved lover
through endless nightsky,
feels the heat,
knows his hunger.
Passion flickers blue,
cold star diamonds.
He holds her waist
lightly, a gentleman.
She is not deceived.
Her lust outweighs his,
her devil,
now and forever lover
who slyly invited her
in from the rain.

She licks her teeth, tears him apart
limb by ancient limb.
His sockets snap
like pop beads.
Lilith sucks,
inhales his soul,
leaves him nothing

but blind faith,
sighs back his breath,
mends him with saliva,
licks every crevice,
deepest orifice
of his lean, crusty body
now clamped upon her fiercely,
a chameleon on a leaf.

27
Lilith and the Gang
Sara Eve Baker

So, we're cruisin', right? Lookin' for a little action, me and my deal, the Fists. Lower East Side. Not our dirt, but sweet enough for a night-ride. Just me, BB, Shiv, Sunshine, and Grue. Spatter's still laid up, knife fight last week, and Meat's in the slam for the job he pulled a month ago. Time he gets out, he'll be so used he won't wanna run no more, with us or anyone. The Man will leech all the bad outa him.

So we're runnin' a bit light, but that don't bother us none. No one'll mix with us, not since Grue did that greaser in front of his whole deal. He's my second, not what you'd expect from a ripper. Short guy, looks almost skinny, with some serious Helter-Skelter eyes. Strong? I guess so. He busted that guy's arm in three places before he tore it off. Sucker was done before he hit the ground. Next stop: a slab at the cooler. Only thing left for him.

I hear the air cut with a blade. It's Shiv, coming up close on my left. She's got one of them Nip butterflies, the kind that swing on two hinged handles, the blade hidden between 'em. She's quick with it, with anything that cuts. And she's got the best eyes: when Shiv closes like that, it usually means heads-up. I check it out, lookin' for what got her stuff up. All I see is this chick hangin' out under a streetlight, holding up the pole.

BB throws his head back and howls. He likes the skirts, always has. He shakes his head, smiles, licks his lips. Just like the uptown Suits, he straightens his stuff, quick package check, and starts forward.

She don't move: it's like the chick don't even see him. I squint, but can't see her eyes; the light paints dark shadows across her face.

"Squeeze, let's hit it," Sunshine says to me. I look at him; he's as close to scared as I ever saw. Shine's a freak, a spider; he'll climb anything. I saw him free-climb seven stories up the side of a building once. Far as I know, nothin' scares him. 'Til now.

Thinkin' ain't my strong point. I snap my fingers to hold up BB; he don't like it, but I'm the one who runs this show. "Shine, watch our back," I order. Without looking, I know Grue is up front, next to me. "Grue," I say, "what's the beat?"

Grue and me check her out. The chick is stacked and dressed for the life: all black leather, thigh-high kickers, not a lot else. Six-pointed star on a silver chain, halfway down her chest. Some tiny tight thing she probably calls a skirt, matching jacket that leaves most of her belly bare. Her skin's so white, light just falls into it and glows. She's got long, straight hair the same color as the light, almost white. Did I say she was stacked? Christ, she was made to bop.

I hear leather creak behind me. It's Shiv, goin' for her backup, a handful of chink-style throwing stars she makes herself. Shiv don't say a lot, but I been running with her a while, and I can tell when she don't like the beat.

The chick looks up, smiles. "I'm Lilith," she says. Her voice is smoke, black as the leather she wears. It makes me think of hot sweaty nights, steam, and sex. Still can't see her eyes. She holds out one hand. Her arm moves like a snake in the light. BB starts forward again. I snap my fingers, he blows me off.

"Yo," I say. I think the skirt's staring at me; she don't want that half-assed deadhead. She wants me. I hook a finger at Grue; he moves on BB, sets him back behind me.

Lilith holds both hands out to me, beggin'. My spit dries up and my whole body gets hard. Beside me Grue turns BB loose. And there's the deal, standin' round like fools. Behind me I hear Shine swallow. We go for it, movin' in on her.

I hear Shiv's star before I see it. It sings past close enough to shave me, heading straight for that pale white throat. Like water Lilith's hand grabs it out of the air, fist tight. She opens her hand, palm up.

I'm close enough to see the star, but it ain't a star no more; now it's some kind of a flower, maybe a rose. I seen roses before, when me and the Fists trashed some old bastard's digs in the upper seventies. Those roses were red; this one's gunmetal grey.

I try and turn so's I can warn off Shiv, but only my head moves. Her eyes are wild. She grabs her other stars and tries to throw, but they're all roses now. And they ain't grey, but pink and getting darker, goin' red. Shiv screams and tries to drop 'em, but they cling to her hand and burn. The butterfly knife droops and curls over her other fist, red as the roses. Both of Shiv's hands are smokin' now. She falls to her knees, her screams catch in her mouth. The red metal spreads up her arms and wraps around her, twining like snakes. Wherever it touches, it burns.

Me and my deal watch this, watch Shiv roll on the ground and choke. The metal spikes off her neck and rears back, then plunges into her mouth and eyes. She ain't screamin' no more. I look back at Lilith. She's still smilin', the rose on her palm gone dead, burnt black.

"Come to me," she says, and we all move together. She opens her arms wide, her jacket pulls back. I want to dive in that skin, touch it and tear it and taste it. I make myself look at her face.

I can see her eyes, for the first time. They blaze red as the roses that did Shiv, red as blood, red as flame. "She got it easy, Hellraiser," Lilith said, her voice whiskey-velvet above the heavy breathing of the men around her. "She only died. You four will serve me. Always."

She closes her arms around us, arms suddenly tight as snakes, wrapping us close to her. I can feel her heat, like I'm shoved up against a furnace. My skin smokes and I scream with the others, pain and lust, endless lust, aching heat. I feel the cooked skin and muscle start to peel off my bones. Fire diggin' deep. I smell barbecued meat. I don't even want to see the rest of my deal.

She turns away.

"Lilith," I croak. She stops at the edge of a pit that's opened before her, glowing orange and hot. Then she smiles and my body leaps. She snaps her fingers at me and BB and Sunshine and Grue. And we follow, down into the pit with Lilith. We know who runs the show.

IV

LILITH AND OTHER WOMEN

If our book is a lively conversation about Lilith among Jewish women, then this section is the whispered exchange of confidences between sisters in their shared bedroom. They love each other for their differences, resent their similarity to one another. They want to help each other, at the same time that each wishes to replace and obliterate the other. They long for Adam, but also long to learn to live without him. They resent their mother so much that they pretend they never had a mother. They can't agree about sex: whether they want it tame, "appropriate," or wild and unrestricted. About children they can't agree at all. But each thinks the other knows something about them that would be worth knowing.

28
The Coming of Lilith

(an excerpt)

Judith Plaskow

In the beginning, the Lord God formed Adam and Lilith from the dust of the ground and breathed into their nostrils the breath of life. Created from the same source, both having been formed from the ground, they were equal in all ways. Adam, being a man, didn't like this situation, and he looked for ways to change it. He said, "I'll have my figs now, Lilith," ordering her to wait on him, and he tried to leave her the daily tasks of life in the garden. But

---

* Judith Plaskow, author of *Standing Again at Sinai*, is a leading feminist theologian. In her 1972 article, "The Coming of Lilith: Toward a Feminist Theology," Plaskow traces ". . . one group's attempt to do theology communally in the hopes that our questions will be taken up by other women and our process made part of an ongoing one." The questions with which the group began was ". . . whether we could find in the women's movement a process, event, or experience that somehow expresses the essence of the movement and that might function as a central integrating symbol for a theology of liberation. . . . We proceeded to explore this question by sharing and reflecting on our experiences as women in the women's movement. We then discussed the ways in which these experiences are similar to or are religious experiences, and finally, attempted to reflect theologically on what we had done."

The group coined the phrase the "Yeah, Yeah experience," to describe the condition of being heard and seen, as the essence of sisterhood; and the making of community as a context for self-transformation. They identified the "rituals" they had developed to express this felt sense of community. And then they set out to bring

Lilith wasn't one to take any nonsense; she picked herself up, uttered God's holy name, and flew away. "Well now, Lord," complained Adam, "That uppity woman you sent me has gone and deserted me." The Lord, inclined to be sympathetic, sent his messengers after Lilith, telling her to shape up and return to Adam or face dire punishment. She, however, preferring anything to living with Adam, decided to stay where she was. And so God, after more careful consideration this time, caused a deep sleep to fall on Adam and out of one of his ribs created for him a second companion, Eve.

For a time, Eve and Adam had a good thing going. Adam was happy now, and Eve, though she occasionally sensed capacities within herself that remained undeveloped, was basically satisfied with the role of Adam's wife and helper. The only thing that really disturbed her was the excluding closeness of the relationship between Adam and God. Adam and God just seemed to have more in common, both being men, and Adam came to identify with God more and more.

---

their collective experience into theology. "What is theology?" they asked. "What does it mean to apply a theological process? Is feminist theology the expression of new religion? How can we relate ourselves to the old without destroying our new experiences through the attempt to understand them in terms of old forms?" The group "... considered what it would mean to write a systematic theology that affirmed the experiences we had been discussing—choosing a philosophical framework, our text, our rabbis, or our saints. But we were worried about the disappearance of the four of us sitting there, our coming together, behind the framework we would create. We clearly needed a form that would grow out of the content and process of our time together." How to do this?

The group realized that much of their discussions had "... many of the central elements of a myth. We had a journey to go on, an enemy (or enemies) to vanquish, salvation to be achieved both for ourselves and for humanity." They searched for a myth. "We recognized the difficulties of 'inventing' a myth, however, and we wanted to tell a story that seemed to grow naturally out of present history. . . . We chose, therefore, to begin with the story of Lilith, demon of the night, who, according to rabbinic legend, was Adam's first wife. . . . Through her story, we could express not only our new image of ourselves, but our relation to certain of the elements of our religious traditions. Since stories are the heart of tradition, we could question and create tradition by telling a new story within the framework of an old one.

"We took Lilith for our heroine, and yet, most important, not Lilith alone. We try to express through our myth the process of our coming to do theology together. Lilith by herself is in exile and can do nothing. The real heroine of our story is sisterhood, and sisterhood is powerful."

After a while, that made God a bit uncomfortable too, and he started going over in his mind whether he might not have made a mistake letting Adam talk him into banishing Lilith and creating Eve, seeing the power that gave Adam.

Meanwhile Lilith, all alone, attempted from time to time to rejoin the human community in the garden. After her first fruitless attempt to breach its walls, Adam worked hard to build them stronger, even getting Eve to help him. He told her fearsome stories of the demon Lilith who threatens women in childbirth and steals children from their cradles in the middle of the night. The second time Lilith came, she stormed the garden's main gate, and a great battle ensued between her and Adam in which she was finally defeated. This time, however, before Lilith got away, Eve got a glimpse of her and saw she was a woman like herself.

After this encounter, seeds of curiosity and doubt began to grow in Eve's mind. Was Lilith indeed just another woman? Adam had said she was a demon. Another woman! The very idea attracted Eve. She had never seen another creature like herself before. And how beautiful and strong Lilith looked! How bravely she had fought! Slowly, slowly, Eve began to think about the limits of her own life within the garden.

One day, after many months of strange and disturbing thoughts, Eve, wandering around the edge of the garden, noticed a young apple tree she and Adam had planted, and saw that one of its branches stretched over the garden wall. Spontaneously, she tried to climb it, and struggling to the top, swung herself over the wall.

She did not wander long on the other side before she met the one she had come to find, for Lilith was waiting. At first sight of her, Eve remembered the tales of Adam and was frightened, but Lilith understood and greeted her kindly. "Who are you?" they asked each other, "What is your story?" and they sat and spoke together, of the past and then of the future. They talked for many hours, not once, but many times. They taught each other many things, and told each other stories, and laughed together, and cried, over and over, till the bond of sisterhood grew between them.

Meanwhile, back in the garden, Adam was puzzled by Eve's comings and goings, and disturbed by what he sensed to be her new attitude toward him. He talked to God about it, and God, having his own problems with Adam and a somewhat broader perspective, was able to help out a little—but he was confused, too. Something had failed to go according to plan. As in the days of Abraham, he needed counsel from his children. "I am who I am," thought God, "but I must become who I will become."

And God and Adam were expectant and afraid the day Eve and Lilith returned to the garden, bursting with possibilities, ready to rebuild it together.

29
Eden

Jacqueline Lapidus

ever since I discovered
Lilith, things
have been different around here

the first time we met
by accident she
came back one night
for a seashell she'd forgotten to pack

Adam was asleep
and I, restless, strolling
in the orchard
climbed the apple tree
for exercise and heard her
singing in its branches

touch me, she said, see
how my flesh fits
the folds and hollows
of your body smell
the flower between my legs
feel my muscles
listen to the life
in my womb

oh, she was beautiful!
I thought I had never seen
anyone quite like her
before next morning, though
bathing in the waves
her image came dancing to me
like sunlight, reflecting
myself

now I go looking
for Lilith everywhere
inventing with her names
for swallow quartz anemone
learning to breathe like
dolphins, laughing as our bellies grow
round as the moon

Adam
notices but says nothing
this knowledge of our power
sticks in his throat

30
Lilith and Eve: Secret Sisters and Successive Wives

Naomi Goodman

L ilith and Eve are forever intertwined, both as sisters—parthenogenic daughters of the Father God—and as opposites. If Eve is the Mother of all living, Lilith, her sister (child of the same father) must be our (unrecognized) Aunt. Their sibling relationship has been seldom discussed, nor has their situation as successive wives of the same man. The sisters represent the two sides of female character as perceived by males: Eve is too weak, while Lilith is too strong. Women would appear always to be wrong.

In this connection, it is important to recognize that all early accounts of women were written by men. The viewpoint of men toward women is preserved in early mythology, in the Hebrew Scriptures, in almost every instance of recorded history and folklore until recent times. We do not have accounts by women to tell us how they felt about anything. We do not know if women had their own creation stories, their own secret explanations of how life had begun. But we do know a great deal about men's beliefs at an earlier time, many of which have been enshrined in our Scriptures and accepted by subsequent generations, even to this day.

Early in the biblical book of Genesis, there are two perplexing episodes. God creates humankind in his image: "male and female

---

* From a work in progress.

created He them," without any technical details of method (1:27). However, in II:18–24, God creates man, then creates woman, out of the man's rib, the first recorded recycling. These conflicting accounts have long disturbed fundamentalists. In an effort to reconcile the two accounts in Genesis, many post-biblical Hebrews believed that Adam had a first wife, Lilith, the woman created at the same time.

The question that concerned our ancestors was why the first wife was not mentioned in the Holy Book. Surely, she must have been guilty of dreadful crimes to have not deserved mention in our Bible. This reasoning could justify Lilith's omission from the Scriptures and explain why she couldn't become the official wife and mother. Thus Lilith had to personify female evil; woman as (d)evil; aggressive woman who will not obey; unrepentant in her untamed ego and sexuality.

In the rib creation, long favored by clergy of all denominations, woman is not created as an autonomous being, an equal, so that the first recorded marriage would be a joining of two individuals, two solitudes (in Kierkegaard's phrase). Eve, the mother of all living, is created to assuage man's loneliness, to be his helpmate. In short, she is the original enabler (in Aviva Cantor's apt designation). Furthermore, she is his daughter, made from his body ("bone of my bones, flesh of my flesh" exults Adam in Genesis 11:23) in order to marry him, thus creating the original primal father–daughter incest. On the other hand, Lilith is Adam's twin sister, a different incestuous relationship.

Lilith doesn't put up with any of this enabling. She is out for her rights. She relates to many other male legends of dangerous women. She is another manifestation of the white goddess, *La Belle Dame Sans Merci*, who appears in many guises in differing cultures. All such mythologies have in common the belief that woman is a powerful threat to poor little man who does not have her connections with the supernatural world of magic and witchcraft, and is perhaps jealous of her power to create life by giving birth (womb envy). Robert Graves, in *The White Goddess*, traces the legends of the witchlike woman to the moon goddess. Her manifestations exist in all religions, in all cultures. She is a wise role model in woman-centered cults (not evil); she is evil personified in patriarchal belief systems, where she represents a threat to man's dominion and therefore must be eliminated or relegated to outcast status. She is the uppity woman, the dissident, the independent, the different, the daring: she is Lilith.

But there is Eve, created to help man, to ease his burdens and his solitude. Now, consider Eve's actions: she is responsible for the first disobedience recorded in the official canons of Western religion. Eve disobeys God's first injunction and brings forbidden knowledge and death into the world. And this is the woman that God made for Adam! *The Woman's Bible*, a commentary written by Elizabeth Cady Stanton and other suffragists in 1895, says that Eve was independent, since she made her decision to eat the apple without consulting Adam. The authors add that Adam trusted her and immediately ate some apple on her recommendation. Then Adam whined and tried "to shield himself at her expense" when God discovered their disobedience, saying that she had given him the apple to eat, and so it was all her fault. In the biblical account, Eve, unlike Adam, does not complain about God's lecture on her sin and accepts her punishment silently. She has been tamed. She is the woman as wanted, expected, and projected by men.[1]

Perhaps Eve was created to disobey, since how else would men have been able to blame women for all the evil in the world? Men maintained that the rib creation made woman inferior, but that was apparently not sufficient to prove her lack of worth. Could it be that God sent the serpent to tempt Eve in order to create a patriarchy on earth in the image of the organization of his heaven? Indeed, some writers have equated Lilith with the serpent who tempted Eve (as have some theologians). The serpent is shown as a woman in most medieval representations of the fall, and also by later artists.

But even the inferiority and errors of Eve were not enough. Women must have been more important in earlier times if so much effort was needed to establish their lower status. The case was not complete. Long before Freud articulated the power of the unconscious, Lilith was created to represent the dark unspoken desires, the unspoken fears, and spoken excuses of men. After all, Lilith was made responsible for men's nocturnal emissions, for their sexual dreams,

---

1. Elizabeth C. Stanton, *The Woman's Bible* (Chester Springs, Pa.: Dufour, 1985).

for the dangers they face if sleeping in an empty house (perhaps because unprotected by the presence of a live woman). Remember that Lilith is said to consort with hundreds of demons daily, conceiving her children, all young women demons, the Lillim, who lust after human men. And recall her hostility to those who did not follow her to the Dead Sea, expressed in her efforts to claim and kill human infants. She is the bad fairy and the wicked witch of all those folk tales. She is the outsider, the danger, the vampire, the bad girl.

Must we not conclude that the Supreme Being could not, or would not, create a woman subservient to patriarchal norms? Since Hebrew men seem to have been afraid that Eve's story of crime and punishment was not enough to keep women in their place, they developed the Lilith legend, which became folk belief. A potent world of mythology and superstition enthroned Lilith as the seducer of men and murderer of infants. A projection of men's fears about women who seek equality, Lilith represents woman as danger. She has supernatural powers, she flies through the air, she finds independence, but only as an outlaw. The cost to Lilith is loss of intimacy, loss of family life, loss of place in the daily community. She represents a warning to women: better be good, as men define good.

Does Lilith have a better life than Eve who, evicted from her home in Eden, lives with intermittent pain as she raises her two sons, one delinquent, one doomed? Does Eve have a good life with Adam, who is exhausted each night from his hard farming, and continues (no doubt) to blame her for his troubles? How does Eve survive the family tragedy when her older son murders the younger and is punished with life exile, so she will never see him again. How does Eve react to her late and worthy son, Seth? Is she afraid that he will suffer the family fate? Surely not an easy life or encouraging example. Lilith, no doubt, has a more glamorous life: one-night stands with demon lovers, daughters who follow her example. An independent woman, Lilith takes direction from no man, but is forever outside of the pain and pleasure of humanity. If there is a moral, it is that women have sadly limited choices.

Interest in Lilith and Eve is not confined to an earlier era than our own. Jewish legends and stories about Lilith rarely mention Eve but in the nineteenth century, Eve and Lilith were considered together. Robert Browning wrote of a threesome: the two women are

Adam's friendly wives, who sit at his feet, while Adam sees through their joint lies ("Adam, Eve and Lilith," 1883).

In the twentieth century, the relationship between Lilith and Eve has intrigued such writers as George Bernard Shaw in *Back to Methuselah* (1921), in which Lilith is the mother of Adam and Eve and is the creative principle that brings the human race into existence. A real friendship develops between Lilith and Eve in Judith Plaskow's "The Coming of Lilith" (see page 166). In *Guarding the Garden* (1993), David Schecter and Margot Stein Azen portray Eve and Lilith as disagreeing: Lilith is the first environmentalist while Eve joins Adam and his male God who believe in material progress. Eve finally recognizes the female wisdom of Lilith and helps convince Adam to help save the world.

The possibility of friendship—sisterhood—between Lilith and Eve is a recent phenomenon, part of the feminist movement of our own time. Why was such a relationship not considered before? Could it be that men were afraid of women's friendships and so gave few such examples in the literature they created? Ruth and Naomi are perhaps the only women in the Hebrew Scriptures who have a positive, sisterly relationship. Other pairs of women, such as Sarah and Hagar, Rachel and Leah, Hannah and Penninah, are rivals in the childbirth sweepstakes and bitter enemies. If women had written these accounts, would the women have been closer and have sympathized with each other? If women were responsible for the legends of Lilith and Eve, would the two sisters have relished their differences and understood each other? Would the stories about Lilith's demon lovers have been believed, or considered calumnies? Might Lilith and Eve have lived together with Adam as two compatible wives? Or could they have had the friendship sometimes achieved by successive wives of one man? Would Lilith have been included in Women's Scriptures as a good example of a woman who insisted on equality?

In our own time, Lilith has gone full circle from evil outsider to recognized role model. Perhaps there is some choice for women, after all.

31
In the Garden
Susan Gold

Lilith stopped her.
"My juice is sweeter," she whispered,
"and my flesh will teach much more."
She pulled Eve gently down on top of her,
slid her tongue across her eyelids,
that tongue which could beat so fast
in the right places.
"Dear sister . . . .," Eve cried
when the pearls of her body swelled
for the first time.
Lilith shed her skin, her story,
wrapped it around Eve.
"It will be a cold journey," she said.

32
Guilt and Knitting
Elana Klugman

Lilith, you and I
    have met before at this crossing.
I envied the way you strode, musky,
    wearing purple silks,
your red hair like flames
    licking the delicious night,
circling so much closer to the moon than I.

You've seen me before,
    invited me to moon dances,
to shout poetry to the stars.
    But I have too often shrunk and shuffled
and turned to Eve on my right,
    gone back to our talks of guilt and knitting,
while you laughed back to those
    who make rules about apples and edens.
Your voice, loud, fragrant reaches me in
    dreams and I am calling to you:
teach me how to talk back.

33

The World of Our Mothers: The Lilith Question

Frieda Singer

"Better to be content as a dairy cow than to be a lost spirit (a Lilith)."
—Bathsheba Singer, mother of I. Joshua, I. Bashevis, and Hinde-Esther Singer-Kreitman. Isaac Bashevis Singer, Memoirs

For Hinde Singer-Kreitman

During restless nights in Polish shtetls,
their bedclothes damp with forbidden
oaths and insights, wives and daughters
dreamed of dybbuks and of Lilith rising
from the Red Sea, of God's ineffable
name.

The unwed were warned that no one wanted
a *chassid* in skirts, and wives longed
only for sons, their daughters sent out
to the wet nurse, where infants placed
in tiny cradles under tables
peered up at a sky of cobwebs and dirt.

I. B. Singer had such a sister.
From childhood she resolved to give up
keeping house to study and write,
but fearing Lilith's isolation
consented to a loveless marriage,
embraced denial.

---

* Quoted in Clive Sinclair, "Esther Singer-Kreitman: The Trammeled Life of Isaac Bashevis Singer's Neglected Sister," *Lilith* 16, no. 2 (Spring 1991), p. 8.

What became of Hinde?
In the grip of what she couldn't resist,
she left her spouse and son to recreate
herself, returning again and again
to live with Lilith's curse.
Her brother wrote of women
obsessed with studying Tanach.

"Nevertheless, if you're willing?"
Avigdor asks Yentl. It's not
what she'd hoped for. She hesitates.
Wishes he'd learn to darn his own socks;
then sit with her as they study Gemora.

34

Dancing-Woman

Helen Papell

Lilith in two-inch heels winged
      as a waltz
   will dance me at the end of days

into the forest I explored
with the Pied Piper
when I was ten. Always now

a map in my pocket: X marks the trunk
hidden under leaves drained
of red and gold. He told me

it held treasures. All that cold October
I limped around it in polio shoes.
I'll ask a key of Lilith. Surely

while we spin
she'll spare one midnight
so I might shake out the dreams

I never leaped,
rolled like ballerina stockings in corners
of the trunk, wide-eyed, waiting.

35
Sisters
Louise Jaffe

Athena meets Lilith quite frequently.
Long ago they were in a sorority
at Sarah Lawrence, Barnard, or Smith.
(You're a smart reader. You deal with
which one. Can't you see I don't have time?
I'm much too depleted from this rhyme.)
They go to the theater, dinner, too
(and only a winner can tell who's who)
where one says "Apple pie's great here. Try it"
While the other laments "Can't. Not on my diet."

They're post-menopausal, defiantly gray
but, like us, they weren't always that way.
Lilith wed young to a Yalie, it seems
for a few years believed she was living her dreams—
Larchmont home, garden, Rolls Royce, the works—
till she became vexed by his sexist quirks.
Then he called their kids demons, spanked them. She fled.
He divorced her, remarried a robot instead
and she moved to a studio—with no regrets—
they let her keep her three screech owls as pets.

Athena prefers barn owls. "Much tamer,"
she whispers to Lilith, then adds this disclaimer:
"Just my opinion." Her owls stand guard
over her many medals she won battling hard
in Nam or Korea. I'll let you decide.
Just make sure your details don't collide.
It's happened to me on several occasions
but, unlike Athena's, my brain craves evasions
nor am I like Lilith blessed with the stuff
that lets a gal know when enough's quite enough.

Athena and Lilith compare notes on men.
Whenever they meet, they hiss "never again."
One's known them in battle; one's met them in bed.
They've agreed it's the same, little else to be said.
"It's much safer with owls," they've both decided.
"They don't make demands; they're not born misguided.
But we have our friendship, a priceless gem
since who can stay sane living with them?"
They grin at each other, knowingly wink
and on wilder evenings sip a mild drink.

36
Sonnet for a Jewish Woman

Shoshana T. Daniel

We share a god whom I do not share. We
touch anyway. *Shekhinah* in our bones.
You don't expect me to know the poems
Hebrew traces on the face of the sea.
I have learned these myths, I tore off my star
of David, whispered: Come to me, Lilith;
waiting for a lover in exile, kiss
of the demons, surrendering the weight
and breath of heaven. Israel: the far
war, borders of Ashtoreh, Asherah,
oranges, sand; so many hands surround
me, skin as dark as mine, more dust than night.
Lo ira ra Ki at imadi;[1]
I mouthe these words in semblances of sound.

---

1. I shall fear no evil for you are with me.

37
If There Were Angels

Shoshana T. Daniel

A good night? I scrape the last of the honey, crystallized, from the plastic container and into my tea. It dissolves uncurling, a flatworm, a snake unfolding itself invisible, permeating the hot amniotic waters of Our Lady of the Poisoned Springs. I lick blood from the cracked scabs on my knuckles, which open when I flex, stretch, unknot my muscles, sway, holding the edge of the counter, clutching something that stays solid in my hands.

We have never quite synchronized, my lover from the lower sea and I. When I bleed, she is dry; when I sleep, satiated, she prowls the building, the landings, the stairs, seeking other lovers in the stacked apartments that loom above the mud—once beach, it has washed away, leaving us facing that expanse of gravel and silt.

I will tell you a story of angels. If they had stayed where they ought, we wouldn't be plowing through them, knee-deep, their tinny, strident voices assaultive as pins, their little fists beating against our ankles as we kick them from our path. They are minute and omnipresent, obtrusive. They crawl between us; their wings are soggy in our mouths when we kiss. Like moths', their wings leave a soft pollen and their legs tread and crawl. Unlike moths, they are drawn to darkness, and to that inner flame that heats, but illuminates nothing.

There was an angel. The Red Sea was her home—she said it was darker and the dancing was better: "In the kingdom of heaven," she said, "the seraphim stepped on one another's feet as they waltzed. The demons had an innate sense of rhythm which the higher orders lacked. And the boy—oh, that boy," said Lilith, "*exactly* in his own image," she said laughing, snaking a lock of my hair around and around her finger, "exactly. Earnest. Ripe for the plucking." But just for the act, she explained. Nothing to do with emotion. She didn't know what it meant to him, how far his innocence extended. "He complained," she said, "he just wanted what he wanted. His good father sent angels to investigate. To knock some sense into me." These angels were named Senoy, Sansenoy, and Semangelof. Sometime in the past, before the dawn of man, Lilith had made fun of Semangelof's name, so he was more than willing to do his share. To the greater glory of God, alleluia.

My lover curdles milk, reaches out for the cow's convoluted guts and sours her insides. My lover strolls through the alien corn and the angels clack and buzz, haze the sun with their chitinous wings. Where they have passed is famine and desolation. When she takes a lover's baby in his dreams and he wakes, discovers the sticky sheets, he rocks and prays forgiveness, as if he'd had a choice. When Lilith tickles a baby, bursts it out in laughter; its mother snatches it to her breast, weeping, cries out: "*Igrat bat Mahalant, Queen of the Demons, keep this monster from my home!*"

"Have I told you," she asks, "of the angels Senoy, Sansenoy, and Semangelof? How they caught the angel Lilith? Threw her down, how she catapulted herself to safety by muttering the magical, mystical, ineffable name of God?" When I roll over, bury my head in the feather pillows to muffle her voice, she peels them back, breathes heavily in my ear, "But have you heard how these angels lifted up her skirts? They don't tell you that part in the Talmud." So once more I yield myself up to her, thick honey of words spreading on my skin, attracting angels.

For her sinful distaste for the procreative, God has made of her a primordial mother. Angels *ex machina, ex dea*, one hundred a day, angels to haunt and shadow her as no child has ever stalked its mother. Is it any wonder that Yom Kippur finds her rolling and thrashing in the desert, screeching, scrabbling at her skin as if she would reach inside and pull out her own bones, fashion of them amulets against herself? Her every act is the antithesis of blessing.

Yet every act is marked by God. Damning her presence, making of her gaze a riot of corruption and dissolution, he implicates himself in her offerings, the bouquet of disaster. Of what is he so fearful? Her disdain, her strength, her lust?—She has forsworn him. But me she loves, me she holds and to me she whispers, speaking my name, a promise and an invocation.

These scratches on my hands—where are they from? And on my ankles, knees ... Clawing through the roughened edges of the night.

Jerusalem boards up her gates, bricks them in with golden stone. Outside the walls they torch the forests, scorch the cedars to the earth, churn the boulders. At the Western Wall the wise men pray, black their heads with ashes. The women have been pushed aside, their little alcoves of ritual usurped. *Real* prayer is needed. And the city shall be as a sacrifice.

A song of ascents. I was on my way to an important meeting in Chelm. I had driven through the day as night encroached, creeping over the edges of the road and spilling my headlights raggedly, pouring their brilliance back at me, a glossy syrup. Suddenly my windshield was spattered with insects. They smeared and splashed and I doused them with fluid, blue-green, but there were far too many for me to use the wipers. I pulled onto the shoulder and climbed from my car, stretching my tired muscles as I leaned across the hood to examine what I'd hit. They were difficult to discern in the half-light. They were not moths, nor cicadas, as I had thought at first. They were too large for gnats, far too large. They were smaller than sparrows—ridiculous! A truck roared past, shaking the leaves of the roadside trees, whipping my skirt against my legs. Then I heard the crunch of gravel, turned to find someone walking toward me, from behind, as if she had been following my car. For a moment I thought I saw a woman dimly remembered, someone with wings. She came up close, and began conversationally, "I imagine that you are on your way to Chelm ... "

A good day? I clear the angel carcasses from last night's dinner dishes. They get mired in the chow mein, the rice; their thin wings tear off upon the sticky rims of the glasses from which we drink our plum wine. There is an angel floating in my jasmine tea, face down. I fish it out with the tea strainer, closing the screened jaws carefully over the tiny, still form. Does an angel have a soul? A corpse? If it is larger than an olive's bulk, has my tea been rendered ritually unclean thereby? What of a devil's corpse? The question stands. When I shake the angel into the trash bag, my whole arm aches, my breasts rub uncomfortably against my blouse. There are disadvantages to demon-lovers: not themselves bruising, they do not know with what ardor they grip. Not themselves bleeding, they do not value the gentle caress over its more brutal sister. Crossing the thin edge to pleasure they scream and snarl, gasp and bite, and their teeth are very sharp.

She must tell me these stories over and over, though I protest that I know them now, hum them as I work, spin their black lace a nightmare across my dreams. "Have I told you," she queries, "the story of the angel and what happened when she reached the Red Sea? Have I told you of the terrible price she paid and the hideous consequences she suffered therefrom?" If I turn away, mumble something, pull the quilt over my head, she drags it down, pushes my shoulders back into the pillow, wraps herself around me like a snake around an egg. She slides against me, rocks her pelvis against my hip and, nipping at my earlobe, murmurs in her thickest Semitic accents, "Let's make love. It would be so good," her "*sooo*" stretched like taffy, her "*goood*" a growl low in her throat. Exhausted, drained, I lie beneath her, weakly holding her arching, straining back. "Please," I whisper, her lips wet, hot against my skin, "just let me go to sleep."

If there were angels who were not also tormentors, I have neither heard of nor met their like. Hundreds buzz about inside the oven, screeching promises of Gehenna and beating their tiny fists against the glass. Lilith twists the knob to self-clean, pushes the button for light so she can watch. Lilith sits on the counter amid the stacked dishes, sucking a section of cling peach; she holds it between her teeth, delicate as flesh. The angels squeal their imprecations as she rubs them in her crotch or drops them to tread forlornly in the can of fruit and heavy syrup. She likes sweets; melted ice cream, rotten strawberries, Cool Whip, boiled sugar. Yet her skin is always acid, burning a hollow of her body into mine as we lie on the fresh-bleached sheets she has taught me to spread to welcome her, and I burn the aloe-wood as did Solomon, not so long ago.

The angels we keep out with mosquito netting. But they, too, have their sharp teeth. Though they are ineffective against my lovely lady Lilith, they tangle in my hair, they follow me to work, they bite and scratch my fingers; they tug at the small hairs on my legs, my arms, up the line of my stomach, around my nipples. I cannot undress or shower until I have sprayed the room with Lysol or Raid. I have tried reasoning with them. I have said, "I have heard the tales you would tell me, the evil disguised as mercy, stagnant springs at the feet of God in the kingdom of heaven. I have suffered at your hands and lived the destruction you perpetrate in the cause of righteousness for His name's sake. I have been cast down from Jerusalem. I have heard your warnings, but they are only words set against the pleasures of muscle and flesh. I make my choice—now honor it!" But the angels will not go. Each day one hundred reinforcements crawl wet and pale from between my lady's thighs, perch for some moments upon her belly, legs, and arms, fanning their milky wings brittle and translucent. As quickly as I kill them, smacking them against the walls and furniture with a rolled-up magazine, another hundred take their place. Yet each night I spread the luminous white sheets, chanting, "I adjure you, Igrat bat Mahalat, Queen of the Demons, et cetera, with the great, the strong, the terrible name, et cetera, that you send me Lilith, daughter to none, amen." Some moonless nights I walk the edge of the ocean, knee-deep, drawing the sea-smell deep into my lungs. The pebbles slip and shift beneath my feet. I swat the angels with my towel and imagine I am in the desert, the wilderness before and after man, no manna, no sweet waters from the rocks. Lilith commands all tides; the ocean foams, it boils, it hurls me back upon the beach, steaming, cuts and scrapes scoring my cheek, my arms, and side.

I am bleeding; blood flows between my legs, where Lilith laps and bites. My neck is bruised and she has flung open the netting, invited the angels to feast upon my burning skin. Our Lady of Steam, Our Lady of Sweat and Sweet and Semangelof. Tonight I made no offering, called no names, spread no fresh white sheets upon the bed but, like the first time, when she taught me how, she has willed herself to join me. I push her shoulders but she holds me easily; I am drunk on plum wine and bewildered by pain. The sheets grow sodden as the angels rub and tear, squirming, ejaculating into the fissures they open in my flesh.

"Have I told you the story?" asks Lilith as I writhe speechless, all words absent from my throat, nonsense and groans, the names forgotten, my own name forgotten. "You will be mother," she says encouragingly, "to a hundred, a thousand demons a day. We will be together always." And she sinks her teeth into my neck.

Jacob wrestled no angels but those who held his tongue, crowded his mouth as he struggled to breathe, shout: "*Senoy, Sansenoy, Semangelof, Adam and the ancient Eve, in the name of the unpronounceable name, out Lilith, amen, amen, amen, alleluia, amen, selah!*"

38
Still Life with Woman and Apple

Lesléa Newman

You have been wandering around Gal's Gallery for barely an hour, yet museum fatigue has already set in. There is a stiffness about your neck and shoulders. Your feet are dragging as if through mud, and your eyes are glazed over as though you have been up all night watching television. You park yourself on a hard bench in front of a painting: *Still Life with Woman and Apple*. You stare at the woman sitting on a maroon couch, one arm resting along the back of it, one leg crossed over the other, gazing at an apple on a small white dish in front of her. Just for fun, you decide her name is Lilith.

From the way Lilith is looking at the apple before her, you know she is thinking about sex. Lilith thinks about sex all the time. Sex sex sex sex sex. Lilith thinks sex once a day keeps the doctor away. Lilith greets you on the street by pinching your ass and asking, "Getting any?" when a simple, "Hi, how are you?" would do. Lilith's philosophy is, straight people think we do it all the time, so why disappoint them? Lilith says if they're going to scream insults at us and throw rocks at us and take away our jobs, our houses, our children, and our lives because of who we have sex with, we better make sure we're having a damn good time to make it all worthwhile.

There's a clock over Lilith's head. Both hands have stopped at the twelve. It is always midnight in Lilith's world, never noon. She is always dressed in black leather from head to toe: boots, pants, and a jacket with lots of zippers, all of them unzipped.

You know this is Lilith's cruising outfit. Lilith can sniff out the new dyke in town just as sure as a cat can sniff out the one catnip plant in a garden of weeds. You imagine her knocking at your door just as you finish unpacking your last carton of books, or right as you are placing the last cast-iron frying pan on its hook in your new kitchen. She has left her Honda purring in your driveway, and invites you out for a ride. Reminds you to hold on tight as she takes you up the mountain to a secluded spot under a full moon and a sky speckled with stars. She teases you with a midnight picnic: "Want a hunk?" she'll offer, holding out a wedge of bread. "Do you like cherries?" she'll ask, extending a fistful of fruit. After the meal, she'll lie back on the grass, her hands under her head. "I'm so hot!" she'll exclaim, stripping off her boots, pants, and jacket. All she'll have on underneath is a black leather G-string and a tiny rose tattooed on the left cheek of her ass.

Her body gleams in the moonlight. "Aren't you hot?" she'll inquire. You try not to let on that you are sweating profusely. Museums are always so stuffy. Stifling. No air. You can scarcely breathe. You loosen your collar. Unbutton your shirt. Shed your clothes as gracefully as a snake sliding out of its skin.

You approach the painting and place your foot on the bottom of the frame for a leg up. You hoist yourself into the portrait and stare at Lilith. She has not moved. She is still gazing at the apple in front of her. Her eyes reveal her hunger. She is starving. Ravenous. Famished. She has been staring at that apple for a very long time.

Just for fun, you decide your name is Eve. You lift the apple from its small white dish, and take the first bite. You chew voraciously until it is gone. Devoured. A part of you. You take another bite, and then another and then another until the apple disappears completely. The apple is now contained by you. The apple has now become a part of you. It is time for you to become the apple. You lie down on the table. Lilith has not moved. She is still still. She stares at you. At your red rosy cheeks, your breasts like two apples, the long stem of your neck, the apple blossoms of your hair. She is hungry. It is midnight. You have never been so still in your entire life. You know you are delicious. You wait for Lilith to take her first bite. You will gladly wait forever.

39
Lilith

Sandy Bodek Falk

Legs apart, I
stand and
the blood that drips

spells your name,
Lilith.
Night falls

And you, with it
climb
hand, foot, hair

trailing out
of my womb. One
strand makes

two. You
born, still
chewing

the umbilical cord.
Tongue
sweet with apples,

your red palm
in mine.
You reverse me,

Mother,
child, you
my

unnamed daughter,
Nazi-murdered aunt,
self. All

night, you
teach me to see
in the dark. No

nightmares, no carrots
in sight. We
fly to the place

before childhood
lessons, before
Eden. Light

breaks. I
wait for no divinity
to trample me

with his white horse. You
cry apple seeds. I
blossom,

grip the bark of
your arms, and
swing myself until I am free.

A Note about Lilith as Role Model

Henny Wenkart

What is the role of role models? Contemporary feminists celebrate Lilith as their role model. But how can this be? She is, after all, not a historical woman to whose life they can point!

Aristotle's advice, which at first reading seems tautologous, may actually be the beginning of role model theory. If you want to know what is the good way to handle a situation, he says, look at the way a good person handles it. Now, isn't that about as circular as any advice that was ever given? Maybe not. A woman who wishes to change the way her self is organized, change her relationships to others, might try to clarify what she wants by constructing a Platonic ideal of the woman she wishes to become. But if she instead tries to follow Aristotle's advice, and looks at an existing figure she admires, even if she is *positing* her characteristics, she has someone to emulate. And that seems easier. So feminists *construct their* Lilith, in the Platonist way. But *they say* that they are merely *correcting* stories told about their "role model" Lilith.

For one thing, if we think something has been done before, we have the courage to think we can do it, too. In addition to this encouragement, there is the comfort that seems to come simply from living through something that a heroine long ago lived through—and this is true regardless of the outcome: mysteriously, comfort comes from reenacting something experienced before—as if it is keeping me company: I am not alone in this. But Lilith is not a historical figure. Hence the companionship felt here may be the companionship of other women who also take her as "mentor."

V

LILITH AND THE FAMILY

Even in early incarnations, Lilith provided a way to talk about family relationships, to express cultural attitudes toward women, especially in their role as mothers. In folk legend, Lilith was a demon who murdered newborn children (unless warded off by an amulet). Thus she served as a projection of women's ambivalence about motherhood and a negative example of what a woman "should" be.

In this section, some writers depict Lilith traditionally, but identify, if only briefly, with her unwillingness to mother. Others see her as a shadowy member of the Jewish "family"—connecting her to Miriam, the Shekhinah, and the First Family. (Eve, giving birth, calls upon her.) Others see her as a "good" mother (or daughter)—in one work, a mother names her child Lilit; in another, Lilith nurtures a tribe of lost children—suggesting that Lilith-like characteristics are a necessary and desirable element of family life.

41
Cain and Abel: A Case for Family Therapy?

(an excerpt)

Alix Pirani

The story of Cain and Abel is the first biblical account of fatal conflict between brothers. It is frequently referred to but commonly misread, and I have often asked myself why Cain and Abel's parents did nothing to avert the tragedy. In particular, where was Eve when all this was happening? It reflects for me our present-day situation: We are everywhere imperiled by wars between men who cannot make good brotherhood, and the women's influence and what are thought of as feminine qualities are apparently powerless to prevent meaningless murder and destruction. This story of the first family seems very much the story of the "family of man"— and I note the gender designated there.

Bible stories have, I believe, a far greater influence on the Western psyche than is often acknowledged. I have explored episodes from Genesis in psychodrama groups and participants have found in them profound meaning and relevance—which surprised them—as well as an urge to change the story for our contemporary context: to re-vise, or re-vision. When I consider the dynamic of the Cain and Abel conflict and wonder whether family therapy might have altered the course of events, I too am endeavoring to change the story. Therefore, I have decided to borrow the approach of psychodrama and write what is my own psychodrama: the female family therapist working with the Bible's first family.

The immediate paradoxes are obvious, and they are crucial. I have to put the family in a modern setting while preserving the timelessness of their predicament; I have to provide mundane versions of spiritual events and deities in human form. I am looking at the origins of a family, which has been conceived as the original family. In effect, I am looking at the way creation led to destruction—and I am seeking a means to re-creation, which is the task of any therapist.

An account of the dynamics of this family and its relationships with the family therapist follows. Basically, the family consists of a "grandfather" (God); his adopted, unrelated grown children, now married to each other (Adam and Eve); and their two sons, Cain and Abel. During the course of therapy, Abel is "tragically killed in a farm accident caused by a tractor his brother had been operating." Cain, who has initiated the family therapy sessions, is undergoing "an acute identity crisis." The entire family is characterized by secrets and mysteries.

When all four met with me again together, I said that I felt there were secrets and mysteries from the past that still plagued this family, and this was making it difficult for me and for them to deal with their crisis in the present. There seemed to be a collusion to conceal the circumstances of the birth and adoption of Adam and Eve, and also events around the time of their marriage. The suppression of unacceptable truths and unwelcome feelings was damaging everyone.

There was a long silence. Then Cain said, "It's all to do with that Lilith, isn't it?"

The old man immediately snapped. "What do you know about her?"

"I've heard rumors," Cain said

"You know nothing about her," the old man said.

"I've heard rumors," Cain repeated. He eyed his father and grandfather scornfully and said, "Is it true she had it off with both of you?"

Well, then, as they say, the shit hit the fan. The mention of this woman, of whom I had never heard, caused absolute havoc, as it later transpired she had once done in person. Eve berated Cain for his disrespect; the old man began a long diatribe on the evil nature of the unmentionable Lilith; Adam grew impatient with him and moaned that he had heard all that before; Eve then turned on Adam and said he was hardly the one to speak, considering his secret involvement with Lilith, at which Adam retorted that Eve was no better than Lilith's underhanded accomplice in mischief and what had that done for them?

Within five minutes the room was transformed and so was Cain, as he saw revealed all the hurt, hatred, sexual anger, viciousness, and jealousy that had lain under the surface for twenty or more years. I saw in that moment that he would no longer need to carry it; and it had taken the death of Abel to release it.

As far as I could piece it together—for almost everything anyone said was denied or contradicted by someone else—Lilith's mother was Adamah (in Hebrew, "earth," "ground"), who had originally owned the land that had been appropriated by the old man, who cultivated his beautiful Eden there. Through his alliance with Lilith, he had taken possession of Adamah's domain—an extensive area largely uncultivated. When I heard that, I realized why he had his paranoid superstitions about the land. Lilith was, by all accounts, a wise and subtle woman, spirited, full of lively vitality, sexually powerful, ruthless at times, passionate in loving, and devilishly cunning—a sort of Cleopatra figure, but with a knowledge of corruption, both human and natural, that gave her great depth and a realistic ability to live and love without high expectations of perfection. That the old man might have experienced this woman's love and then lost her or rejected her, opened up a whole new view of his situation to me. He had lost something irreplaceable, was bitter and vindictive, had banished her from his goodwill, and spoke nothing but ill of her. Yet for all anyone would ever know, she might be the mother of Adam and Eve. Adam, it seemed, did have a relationship with her, but she would not stay with him and submit to the men's regime. She fled—was in effect discarded. She had apparently also led Eve astray in some way.

The secret was out—the secret of this family's disowned sexuality and rebellious creativity. It was a classic case of scapegoating. Lilith had been cast out, taking with her all the disgraced, unacceptable, or shadow feelings of the family, who could vilify her and avoid experiencing their own inner chaos, greed, and darkness. However, she had also taken with her their ability to love deeply and realistically without debilitating superego expectations, so they had all been bereft of a potentially wise mother. The scapegoating had rebounded with a vengeance. In pretending she was dead to them and concealing her very existence, they could not even speak their enmity and fear of her, which would have left the sons free to judge for themselves. Cain embodied all the shadow in himself and acted it out unawares. The unspoken fear, loathing, sexual guilt, and rage, stored up for twenty years, drove him mad enough to kill; and, insofar as the dispossessed Lilith wanted vengefully to kill the men and their offspring, as they feared, so Cain had become possessed by her.

In later discussion with my colleagues, the Kleinian said the old man's reaction to the loss of Lilith showed the classic manic defenses against depression: control, triumph, and contempt. The Jungian observed that Cain had become Eve's animus and was himself anima-ridden. The pattern of scapegoating interested us. This family was particularly adept at displacing its feelings of inferiority on one another and playing victim. Abel was seemingly the innocent scapegoat, sacrificed like the slaughtered lamb, perhaps willingly, to the grandfather. Cain was branded and ostracized for having manifested the family's destructiveness. Eve had been scapegoated long ago by the men for being allied to the sexually seductive Lilith—which was what they had been.

In an individual interview I had with Eve, she recalled Lilith's impact on her. She had come to see Eve when she heard of her impending marriage to Adam. Their father had been telling them how the ideal marriage should be, but had left them very innocent. Lilith's approach was different. "She was like an older sister, or mother," Eve said. "She told me a lot about being a woman—about birth, death, and masturbation; and that menstruation was not a curse; and about sexual love between women, our right to independence, and our right to own land, as her mother had. She talked about sexual maturity between men and women, and about pain. And witchcraft . . . I knew it was scandalous, yet it wasn't. She was very loving and open-eyed and wise. She said the life we led in Eden was all a con. Nothing could be so perfect and I shouldn't let the men dominate me. And my father had as good as stolen Adamah's land and had wanted to steal and possess Lilith also. She said Adam ought to marry her, because if he married me we would neither of us ever grow up. But as she was so much older than him that was unlikely. I was amazed by it all. I told Adam everything she told me. He didn't say much. I'm sure he did have a relationship with her—had already or did later. But he never told me about it."

"You haven't forgotten her," I observed.

"No," she said, "I haven't. How could I? As soon as he discovered what had happened, he was livid. He said she was wicked, a snake in the grass, and I was a fool to be taken in by her, and Adam had been led astray. Adam blamed me, and said she was a temptress and so was I. And we were turned out of Eden and put here in the uncultivated part of the estate. I was very upset and mortified. He had brought us up, after all. I felt so guilty. I let Adam put me in my place, and we knuckled down to work."

"Were neither of you angry with him?" I asked. "Defiant? He must have been afraid of you to want to turn you out."

"No, we weren't as strong as Lilith. And we didn't understand him like she did. And we were too spoiled to want to risk financial independence. Eden spoiled us."

The pattern of power and feeling in the family began to change. As Adam was openly spoken of as a sexual being, his energy and self-confidence revived visibly, and Cain and the grandfather had to respect that, instead of colluding to disempower him. The increase in vitality, which even led to some quite risqué jokes being shared among Adam and Cain and Eve, was a pleasure to see; and it outfaced the old man's killjoy control. He wisely then kept his silence and in subsequent meetings managed to listen to their expressions of resentment toward him without retaliation. He began to look more sad than stern.

In the end, they were able to mourn the loss of the son and grandson and brother they loved, and with that came relief, gradually, from the guilt that had so much ruled their lives. It took time . . . Eve had to work through much repressed negative material and relinquish her power as the submissive sinner. Cain was able, finally, to forgive himself and feel released. He quite soon found a wife and left home. Adam and Eve were released also. She became pregnant and had another son, Seth. This one, I felt, would know who his father was. I had hopes, and still do, that having allowed themselves to mourn the loss of Abel, they might be able to mourn the loss of those blissful days of innocence in Eden and move forward from the guilt about that. However, behind that was a much greater loss, and I do not know whether the old man will ever come to terms with that and stop denying what he lost by casting her out. Eve tells me, when we meet now, that she feels more and more that Lilith was the mother she never had, who came to her almost disguised and unrecognized, and left again. Recently Eve has been trying to discover where she is. The old man let on that she has another name, Shekhinah (feminine aspect of God), and this may help Eve to get in touch with her. "I haven't found her yet," Eve wrote to me not long ago, "but I conjure her up when I need her. During Seth's birth, I imagined she was with me. She understood everything I was going through and her patience and realism helped us both—him and me. I was not being punished for my sins. And even if in my extremity I felt I wanted to kill the baby who seemed to want to kill me, she understood that, too. The men once said she's the sort who'd want to kill her own child. Well, maybe we all are."

When I reviewed the case recently with my supervision group, I was able to report that Adam has slowed down, accepted that they do not have to have everything perfect, and is no longer trying to prove and punish himself. He leads a more leisurely and pleasurable life with Eve and Seth. She has grown in confidence as lover and mother, and has begun to concern herself with conservation and ecology, different ways of managing the land that is theirs without exploiting it. The realization that their patriarch could be sexual and fallible has made a difference to them all.

My Kleinian colleague observed that I had helped the family get beyond the paranoid-schizoid position and work through the depressive position toward ambivalence, which of course involves mourning. The Freudian's view was that we solved Cain's Oedipal conflict by restoring his father's sexual potency and claim on Eve. The bioenergeticist confirmed my observation that the family body, in a literal, metaphorical, and structural sense, had become far more grounded, less top-heavy. By releasing the tightly held pelvis—held by sexual and anal repression—the vital energy, which previously had been directed upward and lodged in the head and shoulders (a manic tendency, precariously held in Adam and Eve but unbounded in Cain, where it went, so to speak, over the top) had been able to flow downward to the earth again.

A family therapy specialist in our group says that for a time I provided the missing mother for the family that had so much suffered from her absence, so that they were able to realize what had been missing and use me to re-create her for themselves. When I see how this family moved through a process of transformation to new ways of respecting one another and that it was the spirit of the scapegoated woman, of Lilith-Shekhinah, that returned to them when they needed her and helped them come to terms with their mutual destructiveness, I feel confident that there is a process we may call love, or therapy, working in our universe. If we have faith in it, it is always available to us.

42

Inside Lilith

Judith Skillman

Forced from the light they come
on slight stems: flowers, animals,
and all the stony, life-bearing minerals,
to answer her with names.

These are the others, the ones
she couldn't steal—babies with wooden thumbs,
saw-toothed Australian fetuses
clawing at shells.

Because another continent could hold the key
to her imaginings, they arrive at her feet,
woman of the original triangle,
girl with a waist more slender than Eve's.

I have to get to know her,
before she takes my children. Already
the youngest is learning about strangers,
coloring gold coins and sugar in a picture.

I have to make peace with her
before she wanders off with my oldest daughter's childhood
and my son's face tucked under her arm, before she enters the room of
  Rachel's weeping

and the river of a woman's hair
borne along by water toward her misplaced child.
These are floods and wildernesses, the areas
she knows by heart massed inside the body.

Her storm-laden eyes wailing in small districts,
after hours. The police cars coalesce,
sending their taut shortwave messages
of laughter and banishment,

but she talks with the light of certain houses
intact on her hair, using her mouth
the way I think she would want it to be used,
saying what I think she would say

after the world had bled from her like sand.

43

The Wellhouse

Judith Skillman

I've come to study
        Lilith's demons, her isolate mating

with the air. A milk line inscribes water
        against the well's stone walls.

I've come in my late thirties
        as bearer of the desolate

child who learns to comfort himself
        with a thumb, a bottle

or a blanket binding, having borne
        a million baby girls

in a space this size, and tied off their blue-black
        cords with my teeth.

I'm letting them back into the structure
        an A frame over cement

where the hole has been drilled wide
        as a dilated cervix

We gather in transition pain
        our eyes unblinking

breathing sulphur, crooked nails
    rusting albinos

all of us thirsty for ice chips.
    The lattice of wood over this hole

was never finished, the window's been smashed
    to let in cats and children

and bleeding women.

44

Kreis

Judith Skillman

"A circle was drawn around the lying-in bed..."
—Joshua Trachtenberg, Jewish Magic
and Superstition

I sweep the house again,
tiptoeing around the human forms
hunched in their chairs, careful
not to disturb the circle of necklaces
on the floor of my five-year-old's
disheveled room.

I break brown eggs,
the speck of blood subsumed by flour.

It becomes an obsession, to catch
the oily crows out tapping their sticks
and canes, birds that walk
instead of hopping.
*
A woman can be big
with a child or a deformity,
and therefore free to bleed. A woman
is a fish out of water, caught between
the kitchen
and the bed
with its little prayer. "Sanvi, Sansanvi.
Semangelaf. Adam and Eve, barring Lilit."

A third of the pie goes, arterial blood
splashed orange against mud walls
as morning advances.
*

In another version the circle is chalk,
the woman too far gone
to use the knife
or the key to the synagogue.
*

If the unborn child is born feet first,
organs pocketed with fluid;
if one eye roves the walls
while the other whitens
like an animal in the courtyard,
if the song's blue
umbilicus lies scattered by the porch,
leftover, uneaten feathers forming a wing of hair,

then it's one of hers, the hundred
born each day.
*

Even as a child I knew she was dangerous,
her scent on the long coats
swallowed up in their little amulets
of mothball.

When the snow
stopped falling my grandmother
lost her breast.

Afraid of her own proportions
she laughs the long laugh
of the crow. The pregnancies begin again
and I am fumbling for antidotes:
belt, or trousers, candle with a string
for a wick. Three angels stand
like sisters-in-law over a sink,
their cataracts intact.

45

Lilith's Loophole

Naomi M. Hyman

I heard you congratulating yourselves
as you snapped your briefcases shut.
You are good negotiators,
but I am better.
I walked out of the conference room congratulating myself.

The thing is, I don't hate babies.
It's just their vulnerability scares me—
I mean, look how hard you made it for me,
born fully formed.

So yes, I break into nurseries like a thief,
And I whisper strength into the minds of those tiny pink girls.
And I unclench the fists of those newborn boys.
And I walk out.

Well, we've got our deal, gentlemen,
and you are full of satisfaction.
But when I promised you that I wouldn't harm the babies,
you left the space of one unanswered question open to me:
Who, I ask you, is hurting whom?

46

Postpartum

Jane Schapiro

> "To her that flies in rooms of darkness—pass quickly, quickly, Lilith."
> —Hebrew inscription to Lilith, the female demon who strangles newborns

Lilith. It's you isn't it,
      casting your shadow across my lawn,
      your nails scraping against my window screen?
You're watching me, I can see
the black coins of your eyes.
Come in, come in, she's waking,
any minute her scream.
Down the hallway, second room on the left,
you'll find the door's unlocked,
I've been waiting for you.

Don't worry.
She's alone.
Do what you do,
but tell me,
I'm not the only one am I?
There must be others like me who
in the early hours
empty their breasts and swear
this is the last,
not another drop more.

How many confessions
have you heard in unlit rooms?
The mother who keeps dreaming

the same dream, her daughter face down
on the ocean's floor and herself
sleeping soundly
oh so soundly on the warm sand.

Perhaps you've seen me
bending over the crib,
my spine arched like a readied bow,
my fingers, feet braced.
We're all the same aren't we?
We come so close, to the almost,
the nearly,
and then that cry. It breaks
through like a cold brick

and before we know it
we're swaying again,
hoisting the warmth into our arms,
rocking, patting, pressing,
humming. Inside worn-out tunes

your name, Lilith, Lilith,
keeps turning up,
a charm spewed from the sea,
a new moon reminding
it's possible, a woman can fly off
like the night heron
in any direction.

47

Lilith Grows a Garden

Julia Stein

I give birth to angels,
out of my ears, my nose, my mouth.
My children find me
seeds, sprouts, twigs,
search for water,
help me grow a garden,
here in the desert.
I've heard stories from them.
Adam got himself a new wife, Eve.
Docile, Sweet. Does his bidding.
My children bring me the lies
God and Adam tell about me.
At night in his sleep Adam's penis
grows erect, wanting me.
He blames it all on me.
He would.
More lies: I steal their children.
Why should I?
I have thousands of my own.
Why should I ever go back there
when my garden is blooming.
In my garden
all the plants, the animals
grow in freedom.

Not like Eden
where Adam is the boss.
Years ago a girl came, the first.
She said she was unhappy back there,
heard the tales about me and set off.
I let her stay.
More girls came. A boy.
I let them all stay.
I see more come.
Three this time.
Welcome to my garden.
I am Lilith.

48
Ghazals from a Demon Daughter
Shoshana T. Daniel

Angels alarm. Their motives are obscure.
Much better than a demon gave me birth.

Mothers, daughters, and their strange relations;
the clash and mesh of the constellations.

Though I don't smoke, I smoke a cigarette
breathe in that ashy breath of my mother.

I am resigned to your silence. Still, some
quiet moments, I ache to read your mind.

Poor Lilith. Legend makes a monster of
a woman daughterless, and unmothered.

Gardening, she re-creates creation:
Our Mother, up to her elbows in clay.

We swap ingredients, a secret code
in which recipes might mean "I love you."

In the old stories, daughters always go.
Why are you surprised? Don't you remember?

I'm so sick of parthenogenesis, I'm
so sick of being and not being you!

49
To Lilith: Considerations on Women, Men, Children, and Thinking for Yourself

Lynn Saul

"Oppressed Hair Puts a Ceiling on the Brain"
—*Alice Walker,* Living by the Word

It's the wild hair that draws me to you.
Snakes, they say, as they said later of Medusa.
My mother lifts her hand to my forehead, brushes away
the gray waves falling over my eye. Last year, she says,
when your hair was short, it was
so cute. I am forty-five years old but she's hurt
when I tell her I didn't like my hair last year.
I like it now. I like the strength of hair,

power that comes from hair
not being oppressed. Comes from
not having to bother. Comes from saying,
This is who I am. Take it or leave it.

They say you ate your children.
Well, some say I gave mine away.
Of course I never thought their father'd tell them
not to see me. But now they see me, now we talk,
and my daughter, who's shaved off all her hair,
is even more like you than I am.

Well, what it really was
had nothing to do with hair. It's just
that you left Adam, and that worried him
and a lot of other men. My problem, though,

is how hard it is to leave. But I find
that a man who likes my wild hair
I have no need to leave.

Aviva says your opposite is Esther. That's the part of me
I never owned. Oh, I once imagined
I could seduce Khrushchev, who looked like my grandfather,
to end the cold war. But my beautiful sister,
who had straight hair in those days,
was the one dressed as the Queen each Purim.
I was wild-haired Ahasueras, with a beard.
I didn't know you, Lilith, then. If I had,
you're who I would have been,
if my mother'd let me.

Of course, in the end the point was
you said God's name aloud.
You felt equal, not only to Adam,
but to God—On a first-name basis!

Aviva says your revolt is "intrinsically Jewish."
Medusa, Lamashtu, Labartu
did not revolt. Revolt *is* a Jewish thing,
although my mother never thought so.

And what I wanted my children to learn
was just that: *Revolt* is a Jewish thing.
Lilith, I always hoped my daughter
would be like you!

50
Cooking a Kid in Its Mother's Milk

Haviva Ner-David

My mother named me after a flower, so naturally she is upset when she finds out I've named my daughter, her first grandchild, after a demon.

I haven't seen my mother in ten years. We fought constantly since I was twelve (when my adolescence and the sixties kicked in—simultaneously, to my mother's chagrin) about the usual things: boyfriends, religion, clothing; and she finally gave up on me when I told her I wanted to marry my non-Jewish live-in boyfriend in a pair of Levi's. Needless to say, she didn't come to the wedding; and she didn't come to see us off when we moved to Los Angeles, where my then husband planned to make it big making documentaries. But we send each other notes in the mail and leave messages for each other on our answering machines from time to time when we know the other isn't home.

For instance, when my divorce (from the *goyish* husband) went through, I sent her Xerox copies of the paperwork, with a note attached: "You were right, it couldn't have worked. He still blames me for the crucifixion." Then, when I found out I was pregnant with my ex-husband's child, I left a message telling my mother that her first grandchild would be a bastard. "But don't worry," I reassured her, "he/she will be Jewish through me!"

The last message I left for my mother was yesterday morning, at exactly 10:47, forty-three minutes after Lilit was born. "Mom," I said, "You have a healthy baby granddaughter. Her name is Lilit."

Well, you can imagine my surprise only five minutes later—when I opened my eyes after dozing off with Lilit at my breast and saw my mother's face staring into mine.

"Shoshana," she addresses me, standing over my hospital bed, her well-manicured hands on her slender hips. Shoshana, a name I had no say in choosing, means Lily in Hebrew. It's a pretty enough name, although I never thought it said much about me. For one thing, I'm not especially pretty, although my mother would disagree; she said I just don't take care of myself—which means I don't wear makeup or contact lenses, or even shave my legs or underarms, and I don't pay much attention to style. I guess if I did care to try to improve upon the looks God gave me—dirty blond hair (more dirty than blond), a perpetually teenage complexion, and my father's (*alav haShalom*, may he rest in peace) hooked nose—I could be more conventionally attractive; but that would be sacrilegious (being that it was God who made me this way), as well as against everything I, a feminist-and-proud-of-it, believe in. Not to mention a pain in the behind.

"You can't be serious about that name!" my mother chides, jumping directly to the heart of the matter, as though we're in the middle of a conversation.

"Quite serious," I answer and add, "Hello," being that we haven't seen each other for so long. Maybe a decade just seems longer to me than it does to my mother, since I've only lived for close to four, while she's lived for at least six. (Even I don't know how old my mother is. *It's not polite to ask a woman her age*, my mother taught me, so I never did ask hers.)

But my mother has no time for salutations. "Who names their daughter after a demon?" she snaps.

Well, I too can be quick on the draw. It doesn't take me long to get back into the arguing mode. Her mere presence does the trick. But I've been preparing for this day. Ten years ago we would have gotten stuck on the issue of propriety: I would have told her I don't give a damn about it, and she would have answered that that's why my life is such a mess. A messy house means a messy life, she always said. But after ten years of working out every scenario in my head, I've discovered how to avoid getting stuck. It's like talking religion—as long as you avoid the word God, you're okay. I'm determined to get through to this woman I can never seem to please.

So, rather than retort that I don't care if no one else in the whole world is named Lilit, I say to her: "Lilith wasn't a demon, Mom. She was demonized. There's a big difference." I feel Lilit release her suction from around my areola, so I rub my nipple against her tiny pink lips to help her reattach herself. Within seconds, she is sucking away again. I chose to breastfeed so that Lilit would never let me leave her the way I let my mother leave me. I want her to want me around. I want us to be best friends. No, twins. Siamese. My mother, of course, fed me with a bottle. *In my day, before everyone decided it's more natural to walk around naked, no one breast-fed*, she has told me. *It's so barbaric, all these women pulling their breasts out in public!*

My mother looks at me now with her squinty hazel eyes, surrounded by blue mascara-thick eyelashes, and waves my words away, like cigarette smoke, with her hand. "Demonized? I could never stand when you used those big words. Speak to me in English. Your father worked Saturdays so one day you wouldn't have to, not to pay for you to go to college for you to learn to be too much of a big shot to keep *Shabbos*."

"But Mom, this is pure Midrash. It's all the rabbis' words."

My mother becomes quiet then. She's always deferred to me when it comes to knowledge of Jewish scholarship, being that her parents were of the generation who were afraid to send their daughters to yeshiva, lest they show up their brothers in talmudic proficiency. When I was in high school, after my father died, I was able to convince my mother that cheeseburgers are really kosher, because the prohibition in the Bible is against cooking a kid in its mother's milk, not against eating any old meat with any old milk. Of course, the fact that my mother believed me didn't change the fact that I couldn't eat at McDonald's. Even if God Herself came down and told my mother cheeseburgers were kosher, she wouldn't care. As long as none of the other Jews in our Bronx neighborhood ate at McDonald's, I couldn't either.

So I tell her: "According to Jewish legend, the *Aggadah*, Lilith was the first woman. She was created alongside Adam. And not from his rib, Mom, and not as an afterthought, but from the earth, like Adam, and at the same time as he was created. Equal."

My mother shakes her head in confusion, but not a frosted hair on her head is jostled out of place. And with her barely lined skin (the result of years of nightly Oil of Olay applications) she looks almost childlike, vulnerable. "But wasn't *Hava* the first woman?" she asks.

It takes me a minute to answer; I'm not used to hearing my mother ask me questions that aren't rhetorical. "Not according to this Midrash." I shift my position on my bed to take pressure off my hemorrhoids and aching episiotomy. "You see, what happened was, Adam and Lilith, or Lilit in Hebrew, argued about who would be on top when they had sex—"

"Shoshana!"

"Really, Mom. I'm not making this up. The rabbis said it."

"The rabbis said that?"

I knew that would get her. "Oh yes. *Aggadah* can get pretty steamy. Anyway, when Lilit saw that Adam was not about to compromise, she pronounced God's name and vanished. Adam was upset about this so he went to God to complain."

"Sounds like a soap opera," my mother says, "your kind of situation."

"Thanks, Mom."

My mother's eyes open wide now. Are those bags I detect under her eyes? I wonder how long they've been there, camouflaged by all that makeup. "So, *Nu*? What did God say?" she asks.

"God sent three angels after Lilith to bring her back."

My mother nods her head now, in her I-told-you-so fashion. "So she learned her lesson."

"No. In fact, she decided to get back at Adam and at God. Legend has it that she visits babies at night and kills them in revenge. But she did tell those angels that whenever she sees their name on an amulet, she'll pass that baby by."

"Oh. So that's what those amulets are for, "she says, stroking Lilit's sparse hair. "Better safe than sorry."

I disagree. I think complying with that superstition perpetuates a dangerous myth. But mostly, I'm agitated that my mother missed the point. "Don't you see? Lilith was no demon. The rabbis created her to put us women in our place. It's their way of saying: 'You see what happens when you vie for equality. You become a baby killer!'"

"Equality." My mother spits the word out like a profanity. "She wanted to be the same as Adam; that was the trouble. Equal means the same, and men and women aren't the same. There's no getting around it, even with the hairy legs." She looks down in disgust at my own legs, which haven't been shaved since I was in high school. "If you ask me, I'd rather be a woman any day."

Holding Lilit now in my arms, her slate-blue eyes staring up at me like I'm her guru or something, I actually agree with my mother. But I need to make her understand that Lilith didn't want to be Adam; she just wanted to be treated like one of God's creations. "We can be treated as though we're equal without actually being the same," I try.

"But when you get down to it, they couldn't both be on top. It's physically impossible." My mother's face contorts as she tries to imagine the scene, and I wonder if Alex Comfort's *The Joy of Sex* diagrammed other positions besides the missionary one.

"They could have switched off . . ."

"So your father and I were supposed to have switched off working at the print shop and taking care of you kids? Just listen to how *m'shugah* you sound."

"Now lots of people are doing it. Some offices even give paternity leave. And besides, this was the Garden of Eden we're talking about. Anything could have happened. Just think what the world would look like now if God had instituted paternity leave right from the start!"

"Paternity leave in *Gan Eden*, I've never heard such a thing," my mother grimaces, although I see her Midnight Mauve lips trying to suppress a grin. "And besides," she adds, leaning closer, "why did she have to leave and go kill babies? She could have given in a little. Maybe Adam just needed a little more time to get used to the idea."

Never before has she acknowledged that perhaps my ideas are worth getting used to. I wonder what's caused her change of heart; but I don't ask at the risk of putting her on the defensive. "But don't you see? She couldn't stay. She couldn't work within the corrupt system; it was against her principles." As these words escape my mouth, I hear pleading in my voice. My own eagerness surprises me.

"Principles," my mother sighs. "It was always principles with you. Tell me what the principle was in getting married to a no-good drug addict. A parasite!"

"I've told you a million times, Mom," I whine. My mother has the ability to make me revert back to teenage bad habits of whining and arguing even when I know the other person—usually my mother—will never be convinced. "Back the we smoked pot, we got high and watched 'The Wall' and sang 'Lucy in the Sky with Diamonds.' If we could have lived our lives perpetually high, our marriage might have had a chance of surviving. It was growing up that did us in."

"Growing up," my mother says, shaking her head. "You call this move growing up? Not only do you go ahead and get pregnant in the middle of a divorce—God only knows how you two could pull that off when you weren't even talking—but then you have to name your daughter . . . that!" She can't even say the name. "She'll be branded for life because of your *mishugas*." That's how my mother refers to the things I care most about: my crazinesses.

"Aren't you being selfish?" my mother continues. "It's her name to live with, not yours. Right, little *sheina meidel*?" she coos at Lilit, kissing her tiny fingers.

"You can call her by her name, Mom," I say, but meanwhile, I'm thinking: My mother has a point there. I haven't considered that my daughter might feel as uncomfortable in her name as I do in mine. It hasn't occurred to me that Lilit might not want to be a walking feminist symbol. Perhaps she'd prefer a flower to a demon. Could I live with that?

"Mom," I ask with a newfound respect for this woman who endured eighteen hours of labor to give birth to a stranger. "When you had me, did you ever think I wouldn't grow up to be your good Jewish daughter with her doctor husband, five freshly washed and dressed kids, and a house on Long Island?"

"You want the truth?" she asks me.

"Yes," I say.

"Not really. I guess I couldn't imagine a daughter who didn't want for herself what I wanted. I didn't want your life to be so complicated like it is. I only wanted you to be happy."

"So I *am* a disappointment to you, Mom. Admit it."

My mother is quiet for a moment; she's thinking the matter over seriously. Then she says "No," shaking her head. "Maybe at first, but now I don't think so. No matter what, you are my daughter. You're still the same colicky baby I walked around the block for hours because that was the only way you'd keep quiet; you're still the same little girl I checked every few hours at night, until the day you moved out to college, to make sure you were breathing. I slept in your bed, you know, that first night you were gone."

"I didn't know you did any of those things, Mom."

"There are a lot of things you don't know, Miss I-Know-Everything-Because-I-Went-to-College. Some things you can only learn from life."

"Life, huh?" I think a minute. If my mother can defer to me on book learning, I guess I can defer to her on life. She certainly has had more of that than I have. So I ask her: "What have you learned?"

"I've learned that the hardest thing about being a mother is knowing when to be quiet."

"No kidding," I say.

"Yes. I know I haven't mastered that completely yet. I've also learned that the hardest thing about being a daughter is knowing when not to listen. Maybe you haven't been so good at that part either, no?"

"Maybe," I say. "So what are we arguing about? You know I will name my daughter Lilit, but still you insist on telling me I'll be sorry if I do. And then you tell me I shouldn't listen to you in the first place."

A wide grin spreads across my mother's face, creating wrinkles, like grape stems, at the corners of her eyes. Even my mother, I realize, can't erase all signs of aging. She's human. "Welcome to motherhood," she says, and suddenly I feel as confused and helpless as I would staring at a dress pattern and a sewing machine. Why is she smiling? I wonder. But it's too late to ask: She's gone as suddenly as she came.

But then I look down at Lilit, who has dozed off and is also smiling; her eyelashes are fluttering, and she lets out a faint sigh, which tells me I must be doing something right. I stroke her cheek, which is softer than the silkiest rose petal, to stir her, in case she's still hungry, and she starts sucking again. Now she still needs me to guide her.

With Lilit sucking away again at my breast, I take a deep breath and settle back into the pillows that are propped up against the raised back of my hospital bed. And soon, I too am smiling. I'm laughing out loud.

"Lilit," I say, kissing the top of her head. "It's all one big joke, this motherhood thing." Her hair is so fine, it feels like a breath on my lips. Everything about her is so perfect and so fragile. I wonder, can I ruin her? Or worse yet, can I break her? She's already so perfect, why would I want to do anything but watch her grow? But then I also know that there's no way in hell I'll be able to be a spectator at my own daughter's evolution into womanhood.

"Well, kiddo, it looks like you're stuck with me—another overbearing mother. And I'm stuck with you, even if you want to register at Tiffany's for your china pattern. Just promise me this: If some day you hate your name, just remember that I chose it because I would have wanted it for myself. Then you can go ahead and name your daughter after a flower."

I reach over and pick up the phone to call *my* mother. This time, I hope she's home.

51
Lilith and Miriam

From "The Imagination of Prophecy"

(an excerpt)

Danielle Storper-Perez and Henri Cohen-Solal

The Origins of the Imaginary

According to the *Zohar*, Lilith was created at dusk on the sixth day of creation. She was alone and could not take possession of her own body. Her solitude does not constitute a meditation, but rather a wandering. She drifts incessantly, seeking a corporeal dwelling to give her shape. Adam's solitude, on the contrary, results from a loss that he tries to remedy, a loss that condemns him to reinvent, to reconstruct, or to hallucinate that part of himself that will forever be missing.

Lilith and Adam are so identical that they must separate to survive, they must remain as far apart as possible. Their intense similarity tears them from one another in violent opposition. The story of the first couple—or the first *non-couple* of humanity—opens on this paradox.

According to Ben-Sira, Adam reacts to Lilith's departure by asking God to send angels after her to return her to him. But she refuses to become one with Adam's body. In exchange for her liberty, she agrees to condemn to death each day one hundred of her de-

---

* Translated from the French by Ilona Chessid

mon-children. In addition, she agrees not to kill babies protected by the amulet bearing the name of the angels who pursued her. Here, she establishes a contract between herself and the angels. And with this contract is born the first opportunity for mediation. But the amulet offers only a feeble promise. It is a transitional object that must absorb, through the writing of the angels' names, the threat of destruction and death. It is linked to Lilith's presence near mothers and children.

We have learned, through the vicissitudes of the exile of the Jewish people, of the dangers that surround begetting and becoming. The longer the Exile endures, the more the men dominated by these destructive forces become dependent on women to assure their perpetuation and their power. Lilith, for them, becomes ever more present and threatening. In this context, men attempt to incorporate women into their own name, as a way of surviving, preparing for the future or protecting themselves. Man attempts, through woman, to regain the path of a *jouissance*[1] that will lead him back to his origins—toward the undifferentiated, the space beyond culture, an inexpressible delight—and this attempt brings with it the anxiety of dissolution, insanity, exhaustion, and death.

The place in which woman is presented as a totality, outside the reach of the symbolic divisions that separate wife, sister, and mother... this is Lilith's place. Lilith... *original mother, twin sister or wife of Adam?*

Lilith, Breath, and Devastation

The *Zohar* describes her, dressed in scarlet, adorned with her long red hair, wearing Egyptian necklaces and all the jewels of the Eastern countries. She drags behind her the madman she has seduced, and, after the pleasure, leaves him asleep in her bed. He awakens to a fiery vision, Lilith in flames, and she points at him a sword raining drops of bitterness. When the moon is in decline, Lilith plays with unwary and lonely men, making them spill their seed in vain. Then she abandons them, leaving them weak and melancholic. Lilith

---

1. *Jouissance*: There is no equivalent in English. The word implies enjoyment that encompasses both possession of the desired object and sexual orgasm.

heads 420 legions; she dominates the other female demons, Agrat, Mahalat, and Naama.

Naama is so beautiful that not only the sons of man, but even the spirits and the demons, are led astray by her. She enters into relations with the sons of man and conceives by them through their dreams. She takes, consumes, and destroys desire and nothing else, and through this desire, she conceives and brings into the world all sorts of demons who flock to Lilith and are taken over by her. Naama, like Lilith, can capture a man's desire while he sleeps in a conjugal bed, and the *Zohar* describes the ritual and the incantation that serves to repel them.

While the man unites with his wife, he must direct his thought to the Holiness of his Lord and say, "Are you here draped in a soft velvet garment? Stop, stop! Do not enter or depart! Nothing of you and nothing in you! Go back, Go back! The ocean rages, its waves are calling you. I hold on to the sacred, I am surrounded by the Holiness of the king." Then he must, for a time, cover his head and his wife's head, and later, sprinkle his bed with clear water.

When, after the death of Cain, Adam understands the meaning of the decree of mortality, he decides to repent. Separated from Eve, he mortifies himself for 130 years, wearing around his hips a rough belt of fig leaves. But every night, Lilith couples with him. From this union are born both a portion of the children of Israel, and hordes of demons to spread confusion in the world.

Lilith, the Seductress, is also the strangler of babies, threatening pregnant women, mothers, and newborns. The Midrash recounts that her murderous instincts are so strong that when she does not find newborns, she kills her own children.

To protect themselves from the anxiety that weighs so directly on their vital force, women hang amulets above their bed or on the four walls of their room. One of the most common inscriptions reads: "Adam, Eve, Lilith, do not enter here."

Lilith, who is not structured as a subject, opens her femininity like a bottomless pit that swallows whoever approaches. Lilith inhabits the space of the imaginary night; she aligns with the reverse side of thought, with Exile, with what lies beyond the self in the realm of the extracorporeal. Many black forces surround this entity who leads a being beyond its limits, to exhaustion or destruction.

Lilith, who presents herself as a space of fusion and annihilation, is defined elsewhere by her rebellion against the fusion of her being with Adam. From this revolt springs the necessity to prolong the world and to give it a meaning.

And yet Lilith, death-dealing and annihilating, represents a force that contributes to the elaboration and dynamic creation of the universe. Lilith—black light, being of bitter tears, desolation, and solitude, the absent presence—can also, where her absence is manifest, pave the way toward knowledge. This space of emptiness, in which breath can blaze a trail, burst forth and make itself known, becomes the space of a deliverance, of a possible revelation. The kabbalistic tradition teaches us that the study of the Torah frees us from anxiety and from the debilitating weakness caused by Lilith. Redefined by the Torah, these imaginary forces can motivate and guide us toward transformation and prophecy.

The *Tikkun* of Lilith

The story of creation opens on a first woman with a veiled name. The story of Exodus, a story of deliverance, learning, and regeneration of freedom, presents us with a new feminine figure, a sister for man, Miriam the prophetess, sister of Aaron and Moses. A kabbalistic tradition teaches us that Miriam is the reparation, the *tikkun*—of Lilith's malaise.

From Lilith, the destroyer, to Miriam, her *tikkun*—What transformation takes us from the imaginary to the prophetic?

Miriam and the Family Story

Miriam is presented in Exodus with a double status of sister and prophetess. She is the oldest daughter of Amram, guide of the tribe of Levi that remained ever faithful to the alliance and to Jochevet. She is her husband's aunt and was called "divine splendor" because of the light that radiated from her being.

At the time of Miriam's birth, the Pharaoh begins to threaten the existence of male Hebrew children, hence the sign of bitterness—Mar—found in the name Miriam. Born female at the point in time when boys are at greater risk than ever, the very young Miriam takes a central place in the history of her family—experienced by the Hebrew people as guardian, guide, and point of reference. Thus, Miriam intervenes to reunite her separated father and mother and to advise her father not to stop engendering children despite the Pharaoh's decree of infanticide. She and her mother save firstborn sons condemned to death. She accompanies her brother, Moses, entrusted to the current of the Nile. Finally, she reunites her brother and mother, and her mother becomes the appointed wet-nurse of her own child. Miriam re-articulates and perpetuates through her desire the "family story." Her desire is desire for everyone, realization of the divine will. This contrasts with Lilith, who acts only for herself when she invokes the name of God.

Miriam, Guardian of the Living

Jochevet and Miriam, associated with Shifra and Puah by the midrashim, are the midwives of the Hebrews. Nonviolent resisters of oppression, they disobey the Pharaoh's order. Miriam, at 5 years old, criticizes the Pharaoh, saying, "Let this man be damned at the time of judgment." Miriam and her mother care for the children, borrowing food and drink from wealthy women and distributing them to the poor. Miriam and her mother pray to God to bring the infants safely into the world so that they will not be suspected of attempting to kill them. Not one infant was born blind or crippled. Miriam is praised for her ability to amuse babies, her ability to practice artificial respiration, and her way of speaking into a mother's ears so that she gives birth easily.

Aaron has already been born when Pharaoh gives the order to kill all the newborn Hebrew males. Amram, chief of the council of tribes, decides to separate from Jochevet. All his tribesman follow his example. But Miriam, still a child, protests: "Father, your decree is worse than Pharaoh's. The Egyptians want to destroy male children but you include also the females. Pharaoh deprives his victims of life in this world, but you, in preventing them from coming into this world, you also deprive them of any future life. Pharaoh has chosen destruction but who knows if his evil intentions will prevail. You are a just man and the requests of the just are favored by God.

Jochevet and Amram remarry, as do all the other couples. Aaron and Miriam dance at their parents' wedding.

The fraternity of Moses, Miriam, and Aaron is the first fully successful fraternity. The Torah and the *mitzvot* are their points of convergence. This convergence neither destroys nor fuses them together; it is their meeting place and passageway. The Name of this passageway articulates Moses, Miriam, and Aaron and drives them toward a mutual respect. Equality leads to reciprocity and no longer provokes fusion. Their equality is inseparable from distinction. Each one a counterpart of the other, they do not become interchangeable but their identities become fluid in a space of transition, a passageway. Each, in the Name, finds his own name without being lost: each moves toward an elaborated, protected, and constructed identity. Through the Torah disseminated by Moses, Miriam, and Aaron, the Creator's plan in creating man, suggested by "Let us create man in our image, in our resemblance" now situates the name of the Creator and that of his creatures without dissolving one into the other.

Lilith bases her power on the confusion between the Name of the Creator and the name of his creations. Taking possession of the Name and pronouncing it allows her, as the *Alphabet of Ben-Sira* tells us, to separate herself from Adam, to obtain her autonomy. But by this very act, she introduces division, by confusing the Name with her own being. Leaving it locked inside her, Lilith becomes a source of destruction, a totalizing space, a devouring creature.

In recognition of the virtue of Miriam, Aaron, and Moses, the people of Israel receive three gifts while wandering in the desert: the well through Miriam, clouds of glory through Aaron, and manna through Moses. When Miriam dies, the well disappears with her, then reappears because of her brothers' merits. When Aaron dies, the clouds of glory disappear with him, then return because of Moses' merits. The articulation of the fraternity of Miriam, Aaron, and Moses in the unity of the Name permits the transmission of gifts that bring protection and life to the Jewish people.

The water from Miriam's well is the water of life, drawn after the close of the Sabbath, when all the rivers have been made fertile. It is contrasted with the water associated with Lilith that circulates at the last moment before the end of the Sabbath, when the souls of the dead bathe and take advantage of a last respite before returning to Gehenna.

Lilith's waters engulf and drag toward death, while those of Miriam make fertile and save.

From the Imaginary to Prophecy

Lilith is deprived of a place in which to be herself. She cannot use her body to define the realm of nonbeing, that empty space inside the self through which another can pass and make interaction possible. Lilith precedes any space of difference in which the space of the self can be constructed, distinct from the other. She even precedes the difference between man and woman. She resides within Power. For Lilith, the only way of being in the other, is to engulf him. There is no space of mediation in which to conjugate the verb "to love." As Adam's double, just like him, or attempting to engulf him, Lilith has no alternative but to flee from him, or to destroy him, inscribing in him her unsymbolized absence, the "black" imaginary. In their failure to confront one another, to exist face to face, there is no space for the word. The meeting of Adam and Lilith can only be the fusion that leads to insanity or death.

In contrast, Miriam guides us toward the space of a dialogue in which each one can recognize himself, amplified by difference.

In this place left to language, prophecy can spring forth, and lay the foundations of fraternity.

Lilith, in her inability to experience fraternity, introduces, by her absolute absence, the infinity of desire.

52

Sister in the Shadows: Lilith's Role in the Jewish Family Myth

Enid Dame

Consider this story:

In the Jewish colony of Nippur in ancient Babylonia (sixth century C.E.), a man experiences an erotic dream. The seductive woman in his dream is decidedly not his wife. Yet she apparently has some sort of conjugal rights over him, some expectations. She has visited him on other occasions, often in the company of various male and female companions. Waking, the man knows he must end this illicit relationship. Furthermore, he knows exactly how to accomplish this aim: he must consult a rabbi and procure a *get*, a letter of divorce. Only then will his persistent visitor leave him alone.

We can imagine what the text of this legal document might say because examples have come to light from an excavation in Hilla, in modern Iraq. These are in the form of bowls inscribed with Aramaic text, sometimes accompanied by a sketch of the chief female seducer: a woman with long hair, sharp breasts, conspicuous vagina, and bound ankles. All of the dream-visitors are named, not as individuals, but by category: the males, reflecting their Sumerian origins, were called Lilin, or storm-demons. The women were called by the female form of the same word: Lilith.[1]

---

1. Raphael Patai, *The Hebrew Goddess* (New York: Avon, 1980), p. 185.

In one inscription, for example, a group of demons visiting both a husband and a wife are informed "that Rabbi bar Perahia has sent the ban against you . . . a divorce writ [*gita*] has come down to us from heaven, and therein is written your advisement and your intimidation, in the name of Palsa-Pelisa ["Divorcer-Divorced"]"[2].

What does it mean to divorce oneself from a dream partner, to obtain a legal separation from one's fantasies? How does a contemporary reader read this text? The divorce-bowls are intriguing because they imply an unusual degree of interpenetration, or collaboration, between the forbidden and the normative, the real and the unreal, the world where fantasy lovers invade dreams, and the world where men and women marry and divorce. A reader who knows her Freud may smile at this charmingly transparent bit of folk psychology. But this story raises additional questions for those interested in the evolution of the Lilith myth. The divorce-bowls are significant because they reveal that, even in the sixth century, long before what Lilly Rivlin calls the "official myth" of her character and narrative was in place, before her identity as a specific, distinct woman had coalesced out of fragments of Sumerian cosmological legends, Babylonian mythology, and Jewish folktales, the figure of Lilith assumes what would become a familiar role: a woman operating both inside and outside her culture, a demonic invader who nonetheless makes the claims of a wife, who is subject to, and accepts, the laws of her community.

Certainly, the figure of Lilith has long held great emotional and cultural significance for Jews. Mentioned sketchily in the Talmud as a long-haired, winged demon, her story takes on structure and resonance in *The Alphabet of Ben Sira*, a Hebrew Midrash of the Gaonic period (probably eleventh century):[3] In this version, Lilith, created to be Adam's first wife, confronts her husband over a very contemporary issue: gender politics. Adam insists she lie beneath him in the sexual act; as a male, he implies, he is entitled to dominate her. She resists, arguing logically that, since both were created out of mud, they must be equal. When Adam refuses to concede, she utters God's

---

2. Ibid., p. 186.
3. Dates for this text vary wildly. Aviva Cantor places it somewhere between 600 and 1000 C.E. Raphael Patai has placed it in the eleventh century. See *Gates to the Old City* (New York: Avon, 1980), p. 261.

"Ineffable Name," and voluntarily leaves Eden for a home by the Red Sea. Adam begs for her return; God sends three angels, Senoy, Sansenoy, and Semangelof, after her, but she defies them. Eventually, however, an agreement is reached: Lilith will not return to Adam, and will refrain from killing children if an amulet is employed. And one hundred of her own (demon) children will die each day. The first marriage is dissolved.

In Kabbalah, the medieval Jewish mystical body of writing, Lilith's story will take on cosmic proportions. (Once considered heretical, this mystical tradition recurs throughout the centuries, although it is not accepted by mainstream Judaism.) She will emerge as the wife of Samael (Satan), and therefore, the Queen of the Realm of the Force of Evil, or the Other Side (*sitra ahra*). In the *Zohar*, the central text of this tradition, she will be depicted as a sexual temptress of incredible powers, whose charms entice an entire gallery of heroes and patriarchs (wily Jacob resists her advances, wine-tippling Noah succumbs, experienced Solomon dominates their relationship). Here she will be counterposed to the *Shekhinah* or *Matronit*, the feminine, maternal aspect of God envisioned by the kabbalists. The language applied to her grows lush and inflammatory: she's compared to an "abhorrent prostitute," described as "filth," and addressed as "Excrement!" The details of her appearance are minutely recounted: she wears a purple (or red) dress; her hair is long, red, and artfully arranged; she is adorned with jewelry; "six trinkets dangle from her ears."[4] Paradoxically, in the *Zohar* Lilith attains her most exalted position as mistress of God in the absence of the *Shekhinah*, his divine counterpart and mate, who leaves him alone to follow the Jewish people into Exile after the destruction of the Temple.

Citing Lilith's history from her earlier role in the Sumerian Gilgamesh epic (2400 B.C.E.) to her appearance in Kabbalah, Raphael Patai declares, "There can be little doubt that a she-demon who accompanied mankind—or at least a part of mankind—from earliest antiquity to the threshold of the Age of Enlightenment must be a projection, or objectification, of human fears and desires."[5] What ex-

---

4. David Chanan Matt, trans., *The Zohar: The Book of Enlightenment* (New York: Paulist Press, 1983), p. 77, p. 88, p. 78.
5. Patai, *Hebrew Goddess*, p. 222.

actly are these "fears and desires"? Undoubtedly, Lilith is an expression of male fear of female autonomy, assertion, and sexuality. Women, as Aviva Cantor suggests, may have, even in ancient times, found some aspects of her story—her independence, strength, and courage—admirable and empowering.[6] Contemporary feminists have reacted to her with enthusiasm, reinterpreting her most salient characteristics—boldness, rebelliousness, overt expression of sexuality—as heroic, rather than demonic.

Obviously, there are many ways to read—and revise—the Lilith story. One aspect, or "reading," that I wish to explore here is Lilith's role in the creation and maintenance of the Jewish family—or rather, in the Jewish family's idea of itself. For, to a great extent, I suggest, the figure of Lilith has been, and remains, a way of talking about that family: what it values; how it sees women; what it wishes to acknowledge; what it cannot, finally, do without.

It may seem bizarre to speak of Lilith as a member of the family. Isn't she, after all, the original outsider, the woman who walked away, who, in Barbara Koltuv's words, "chooses the wilderness"?[7] Isn't she excised from Scripture—except for one reference in Isaiah, often translated as "Screech Owl"—as she is barred from certain rooms? Yes, one could argue, but she keeps coming back: Talmud, traditional Midrash, kabbalistic writings, and contemporary midrashic prose and poetry all document her complex relationship with her community. It is common to refer to her as an "outcast," but that term isn't completely accurate. For she is not, in fact, cast out, but instead relegated to the margins of the culture. In spite of all the incantations, amulets, divorce decrees, and cautionary tales about her, Lilith never entirely disappears. I suggest that she cannot be banished because she is needed. She is part of the family. Like that of every family member, her role is distinct and necessary. Without her, the family could not function.

The stories that a culture tells itself, whether oral or written, sacred or secular, reinforce its expectations. Jewish culture provides many examples of such stories. One obvious instance is the part of the Passover ritual in which the Four Sons—good, wicked, simple,

---

6. See pp. 15–22.
7. Barbara Black Koltuv, *The Book of Lilith* (York Beach, ME: Nicolas Hays, 1986), p. 24.

and too young to understand—are identified and literally written into the ceremony. The contrast between the good son, who is an intelligent participant, and the bad son, who separates himself from his family and their observance, is quite forceful; its implications extend beyond the Seder: good sons participate in the maintenance of their religious traditions, bad sons opt out. Similarly, Lilith may operate in the culture as the supreme example of a bad girl, a bad wife, a wicked daughter. Cantor suggests that even though the original stories about Lilith (which may have been oral folktales, told by women) were a probable source of female empowerment, these were rewritten by Jewish men in the late Middle Ages, a time of great danger and anxiety for Jews, into cautionary tales featuring a paradigm of female evil. Men insecure about Jewish survival, anxious about their own lack of status, might well have feared the example of a woman who refuses to nurture, feels free to leave, and refuses to let them control the sexual act and the means of reproduction. (In some tales, Lilith steals semen from sleeping men.) In such a psychological situation, women too must be made to see Lilith as demonic; hence, the proliferation of stories about her child-killing activities.[8]

Apparently, it isn't enough to command women to be "good"; a "bad" role model must also be present as a negative example, or projection, of the culture's worst fears. A personified dichotomy between "good" and "bad" figures recurs throughout Jewish texts, sometimes in unexpected ways. Thus, Lilith is sometimes paired by modern commentators not with Eve, as might be expected, but with Miriam. The connections between these two women are intriguing: both are strong-minded, outspoken, and rebellious (one meaning of Miriam's name); both are associated with the births and deaths of children, and with water, particularly the Red Sea. Both endure and survive punishments inflicted by God. Both are, in different ways, ultimately marginalized. Yet the contrasts are even sharper: Lilith's role in the culture is a "shadow" one. Miriam is an integral part of Jewish history.

A cosmic dichotomization between Lilith and another female figure, of course, occurs in the *Zohar* where Lilith, the eternal seductress and Queen of the Realm of Evil, is contrasted with her ap-

---

8. Cantor, see pp. 15–22.

parent opposite, the *Shekhinah*. But this contrast is not a simple one.

In one particularly significant passage from the *Zohar*, Jews are instructed about preparing their houses for the Sabbath. The house is to be made lovely, as if for the reception of a bride—the personification of the Sabbath herself, often called the *Matronit*, another name for the *Shekhinah*. Cushions, candles, attractive clothes, and household adornments are to be employed; a special seat, comfortable and resplendent with embroidered cushions, is to be set aside for "the Lady." Yet there is another woman in the picture: Lilith, "the Evil Handmaid," is also present "in the dark, hungry, crying and wailing, wrapped in mourning clothes like a widow . . . without her husband, without a chariot" The two female forces are specifically contrasted: "when the one is fulfilled, the other is destroyed."[9]

How might a contemporary reader interpret this scene? First, it seems significant that Lilith is depicted as a widow (or "like" one): a woman who has suffered a loss. The designation does not suggest a solitary, extra-human figure, but a woman capable of making ordinary connections, experiencing ordinary emotions. Also, her pose is not threatening; rather, it is one that might elicit compassion. Is she expressing a wish to be included in the festivities? Or grieving for a lost attachment? In either case, it would seem she is not alien to this community, but rather has some sort of claim on it.

Furthermore, in spite of the text, she is not actually "destroyed." She is not even banished; she does not leave the house, or even the room. She simply retreats to the shadows. Clearly, she is part of the scene.

One wonders: Why is she there? Does the Bride need the widow, her shadowy counterpart? Can the Sabbath feast take place without both women's presence? Is this a simple contrast between good and evil: the honored, indeed, divine, female guest given a seat in the spotlight, the transgressive sister relegated to the shadows? We contemporary feminist readers might tend to dismiss this text at first as a simple exercise in medieval misogyny. But should we do this? The woman in the shadows, after all, is the woman who knows God's secret name. She is a powerful, attractive presence who can give comfort even to God, in his male form, when the *Shekhinah* has "aban-

---

9. Patai, *Hebrew Goddess*, pp. 240–241.

doned" him. What she represents is profoundly desired, or needed, even when it cannot be acknowledged.

In this way, Lilith is like the child who plays a special role in the family: the one who embodies or expresses the family's pain, rigidly suppressed secrets, and inability to function. The unspoken family contract: to project its rage or unhappiness or unacceptable impulses onto this child, who having no choice, "accepts" the role, and may even fulfill it creatively. In a physically abusive family, this may be the one child who is repeatedly punished for transgressions tolerated or ignored in the other siblings. In other families, the dynamic is psychological. One child in an otherwise "perfect" family may be seen—may come to see herself—as the bad girl, the wild girl, the embarrassing girl, the girl who must be kept in the shadows. Paradoxically, she may be receiving odd, contradictory messages from her parents, who, in some ways, may identify with and encourage the behavior they officially denounce.

Often she is the one who knows the family secrets ("the secret name of God"): the father's bouts of drinking, the mother's suicide attempt, the aunt's mental breakdown. She may at times serve as the confidante of one, or both, parents. She may be her father's "little buddy," his "partner," with whom he (sometimes) shares knowledge, camaraderie, and jokes. (At its most extreme, as Sue Burton suggests, this dynamic may be literally incestuous.) Yet when she begins to express her own sexuality, to go on dates, come home late, embrace her boyfriend openly, her father may label her a "whore." Or, she may be her mother's "best friend," receiver of confidences about the older woman's unfulfilled life, mistreatment by men, difficult pregnancies, disappointing children. This mother may be shocked when her daughter does not duplicate her own life, but rejects marriage, sex with men, and children. "You're sick," she may say. "Unnatural. Normal women marry."

This girl may leave home early, "hungry" for experience. She may become the woman with a string of unhappy, complicated relationships with men, all of whom she has to abandon; the woman who arrives at family gatherings with a brood of messy, noisy children in tow. Or she may be the lesbian daughter who invites her woman lover to the Seder. She is the daughter around whom family fights coalesce at the inner table, the lightning rod for the sizzle of emotions usually kept in check. The other family members deplore her—

to them—disorderly or dangerous life. But they keep inviting her back; she keeps accepting. Indeed, they must invite her; she must accept. The family rituals cannot take place without her.

I suggest that Lilith plays a similar role in the Jewish family myth, the daughter who stretches the boundaries of acceptable experience but who never breaks her bonding with the family. But the mythic narrative, as recounted in the *Zohar*, is even more complicating. It allows for Lilith, the bad woman, to be not only contrasted with the *Shekhinah*, her virtuous opposite, but at times conflated with her, as in the following passage: "Come and see: the *Shekhinah* is at times called The Mother, at times the Slave-Woman [i.e., Lilith] at times the King's Daughter." In another passage, Lilith is described as "the 'nakedness' of the *Shekhinah*."[10] This association of two apparently opposing female forces might suggest, as Patai puts it, that, "since circumstances constantly change, the goddess [can appear] once as good and once as evil."[11] I suggest that this conflation can also imply that whatever Lilith represents may be neither good nor evil in itself, but rather, an essential aspect of life in its divine and human forms.

Contemporary Jewish women writers have no problem identifying with, rather than rejecting, their own Lilith-like impulses. Recently, there has been a virtual outpouring of poems and Midrash about Lilith. While some women writers repeat the traditional representation of Lilith as a transgressive woman, there is a new element: it is clear that the writer identifies, if only momentarily, with Lilith's transgressions. Jane Schapiro, in her poem "Postpartum," for example, recounts with chilling economy a mother's sudden, destructive emotion.

More surprising are a number of poems in which Lilith is portrayed as a good mother, a parent who gives her daughter permission to explore her own "wilderness." Evidently, many women wish for a Lilith-like parent, or hope to transmit Lilith-like qualities to their daughters. These women poets have formulated some interesting ways to talk about the complex, problematical mother–daughter bond.

---

10. Ibid, p. 218.
11. Ibid.

It is a truism that motherhood in our culture (as in virtually every other) comes equipped with a vast load of ideological baggage. Our mothers are frequently represented as self-sacrificing nurturers; dominating witches ("castrators"); efficient, antiseptic June Cleavers; or rigid enforcers of conventional gendered behavior. Mother is rarely depicted as a wild woman; wild women are by definition bad women; good mothers cannot be bad women. But some midrashic poets can and do imagine Lilith as both wild woman and successful parent.

For example, Julia Stein, in her jaunty poem "Lilith Grows a Garden," recreates Lilith as a female Peter Pan, a proprietor of a garden-sanctuary for runaway boys and girls. Shoshana Daniel explores what she calls "the clash and mesh of the constellations" in "Ghazals for a Demon Daughter." The speaker here clearly wants her mother to be a Lilith-figure, a demon. This mother–daughter relationship, though filled with conflict, is acceptable to the speaker because it is clearly defined.

In Lynn Saul's "To Lilith: Considerations on Women, Men, Children, and Thinking for Yourself," several conversations are in progress. One is between the middle-aged speaker and her mother, a conventional Jewish woman; one between the speaker and Lilith, her long-haired heroine; and a third between the speaker and her own rebellious daughter, "who's shaved off all her hair." The poem wittily examines different ways of being a parent, a woman, and a Jew. Reclaiming the tradition of Jewish resistance for herself—"Revolt is a Jewish thing, although my mother never thought so"—the speaker implies she is acting as a good Jew *and* a good mother when she passes this tradition on to her child: "Lilith. I always hoped my daughter would be like you."[12] This poem is not merely about Jewish revolt and female autonomy; it is also an expression of a woman's longing for a blessing from a mother who understands her need to define herself.

The issue of a parental blessing reappears in Helen Papell's "Achsah at the Spring," a beautifully textured, resonant poem. Papell transforms the brief story of Caleb's daughter, in Judges, into a powerful fantasy of women maintaining life-affirming bonds in a sick, ruptured world of aggressive male warriors. According to the bibli-

---

12. See pp. 281–84.

cal text, Caleb, who is Miriam's husband, gives Achsah in marriage to his nephew Othniel, as a reward for prowess in battle. Achsah asks her new husband to demand a field of her father. He does so, the field is given, but it is infertile south land. Achsah then travels to Caleb's house to ask for both a blessing and a functioning spring. In the scriptural text, this episode is framed by graphic accounts of slaughter and mutilation, as Jacob's descendants and their tribes fight desperately to subdue Canaan. The poem begins:

> The spring my father gave me
> weeps like Lilith searching for her daughters.
> Here, mothers scrub blood from battle clothes.
> The water stumbles red.

Papell is evidently making use of the Midrash in which Lilith is punished for leaving Adam by giving birth to, and losing, one hundred demon children each day. The implications of this story are tragic, yet few commentators, including contemporary feminists, express empathy for Lilith's plight. Perhaps this is owing to the sheer hyperbole of the situation: it is difficult to feel anything but astonishment at the huge number of demons produced and destroyed daily. Too, these progeny are seldom personalized or assigned genders; they seem literally inhuman, larger-than-life, an amorphous mass of energy. Papell deftly scales down this drama, making the number of lost children small enough to "search for," and gendered ("daughters"). This reading of the story links Lilith to other bereaved maternal figures: Niobe, Hecuba, and most particularly, Demeter, a powerful mother unable to protect her daughters. In addition, Lilith is (once again) connected to Miriam, Achsah's mother, here not depicted as a prophet, but as a "slave-mother" who produced water miraculously on the desert. Achsah, like her mother, wants to provide sustenance; she asks Lilith for a blessing to help her fields grow "so the land may have peace."[13]

While this poem clearly draws on Lilith's earlier incarnation as a Sumerian goddess-figure, it is primarily as a mother that Achsah turns to her. Not only is Lilith here connected with various mothers from Greek mythology and history, with Achsah's mother Miriam of the

---

13. See pp. 363–66.

life-sustaining well, and the community of mothers with dead or wounded sons, but the blessing Achsah asks of her is obviously meant to be contrasted with the original blessing asked of her father. Both requests ask for the same thing: assistance in making a barren field productive. As Father Caleb's blessing came tainted with his ideology of conquest, it is ineffective: the spring, once granted, turns red with the blood of slain soldiers. Achsah must turn to a mother-figure, a woman, Lilith, who embodies a different sort of power.

In many ways, "Achsah at the Spring" is a paradigm of contemporary feminist midrashic poetry. In the scriptural text, Achsah's story is a brief domestic episode in a history of conquest. Papell's retelling gives it centrality and significance; it becomes a commentary on that history and a meditation on the possibility of an alternative vision. It is interesting to note that Lilith's role here is both shadowy—she remains offstage; the poem is, after all, about Achsah—and powerful.

The weeping woman hidden in the dark corner of the room in the Zoharic passage has become an unseen, but deeply felt, maternal presence. Apparently, female attributes considered threatening to sons may well be empowering to daughters.

VI

LILITH AS ARCHETYPE, FEMALE PRINCIPLE

Lilith as archetypal seductress, who stole children from their cradles and robbed sleeping men of their semen, has been the product of the male imagination and psyche for many centuries. But what happens when the patriarchal religious and cultural canons are challenged? What are the consequences of women's imagination loosed and unfettered? Wow! Just as the dream of one individual is said to be part of the unconscious individual myth, so the myth of a whole people—or a gender, as it were—can be described as the dream of a collective.

From the depths of their dreams and unconscious and real experiences, the women in this chapter have re-imaged and re-imagined Lilith as the archetypal female principle. Lilith is everywhere. For one writer, a "conscious knowledge" of her is vital to spiritual and psychological development; for another, Lilith is the omniscient Creator; elsewhere she is the key to a "new world"; she is the nocturnal visitor to a meditator reflecting on a Koan; for a passenger on Noah's ark she is the omniscient spirit "sighted starboard"; she is the spirit of the Torah, the Sabbath bride; and she is with Aschsah at the spring praying for peace. She is everywhere hailing a new consciousness. And this is only the beginning.

53

Barbara Black Koltuv's
The Book of Lilith:
A Summary

In 1986, Koltuv, a clinical psychologist and Jungian analyst, collected the sources of the Lilith legend in her groundbreaking work *The Book of Lilith*. Koltuv brings a long-needed psychological insight into Lilith as an archetype:

> Lilith is something of a renegade instinct sent by God, to exist in the lower regions, i.e., in relation to humankind. Men experience her as the seductive witch, the death dealing succubus, and the strangling mother. For women she is the dark shadow of the Self that is married to the devil. It is through knowing Lilith and her consort that one becomes conscious of one's Self.

Koltuv sees Lilith as both a personal and a collective feminine shadow who has been suppressed or cast out by the traditional patriarchal mode. Dr. Koltuv writes that a . . . "conscious knowledge of this connection to Lilith and the Goddess is vital to woman's spiritual and psychological development."

The war between Eve and Lilith rages within, Koltuv holds. While Judith Plaskow and Naomi Goodman and several poets have created

---

* We wanted to include an excerpt from Barbara Koltuv's *The Book of Lilith* in this anthology. However, her book does not lend itself easily to excerpting. Therefore, with Dr. Koltuv's permission, we are presenting a summary of her book.

new midrashim, which have Lilith and Eve coming together as "sisters," Koltuv's psychological approach to the development of feminine psychology presents Lilith and Eve as interior parts of the feminine self, which must be integrated.

Both "Lilith and the *Shekhinah* follow in the footsteps of the flock, are black but comely, and are experienced by women as aspects of the transpersonal shadow." How do they differ from Eve?

> Eve can have her needs met in a relationship. Lilith cannot. She must cut and run. She refuses dependency and submission. She will not be bound or pinned down. She needs to be free, to move, and to change. She is an aspect of the individuating feminine ego that can only develop in the wilderness, unrelated, without Eros and childless, ever jealous of Eve who remains in man's embrace.

How can they move toward an integrated Self?

> It is necessary for a woman to listen to her Lilith needs for freedom and isolation, to strangle her infantile needs for love and approval within a relationship, and to flee from the needs of others.
>
> Lilith's child-killing energies can be redeemed through conscious reflection on her nature. Again, a mirror is required to know the Lilith quality and transform it from self-destructive killing to self-acceptance and loving.
>
> Thus, the Solomon-like wisdom of the heart connects a woman to her own feminine nature, which contains both Lilith and Eve and prevents her from becoming wholly possessed by Lilith's demonic power-seeking destructiveness.

"It is this Solomonic wisdom," Koltuv writes, "mirroring the woman's divine and demonic nature, that redeems Lilith. She cannot be cast out; instead, she must be called in and known consciously.... A high level of consciousness [is] necessary for a successful encounter with her."

At the end of her book Koltuv makes four points about Lilith's qualities:

> Lilith is that part of the Great Goddess that has been rejected and cast out in post-Biblical times. She represents the qualities of the feminine Self that the Shekhinah alone does not carry. The first of these qualities is lunar consciousness, which is a connection to the cycles of waxing and waning: life, death, and rebirth; and the Goddess as

maiden, mother, and crone. Lilith the Younger is Naamah, the maiden and seductress. Lilith the Ancient One is child killer, hag, and snatcher, while Lilith, herself, is the "mother of the mixed multitude," the Goddess of Life and Death, and the flame of the revolving sword.

The second rejected quality of the Goddess that Lilith represents is the body—instinctuality, and sexuality. In patriarchal times, woman is seen as vessel and mother, her sexuality is limited to the proscribed marital embrace, or idealized and spiritualized into Virgin and "Spacious as the Skies." Lilith is neither. She is whore and earth. Her sexuality belongs to herself and to the Goddess.

Third, both Lilith and the *Shekhinah* represent the rejected Goddess's quality of prophetic inner knowledge and experience over logic or law. Because Lilith wanders in the footsteps of the flock as the darkest shadow of the Self, she is directly felt and experienced within oneself, unmediated by word or law. Lilith knows the magic name of God, and dares to use it in her flight from Adam. Lilith is a younger aspect of the Goddess and does not have to wrest the power of the word from the father Gods. She already knows it.

The fourth and final feminine quality carried by Lilith is that of God the mother and creatrix, in addition to God the father and creator. In this sense, Lilith is Adamah, the feminine red mother earth of woman's nature. She is the part of the feminine Self that modern woman needs to reconnect with in order to no longer be a spiritual outcast. Lilith can help women remember that.

Koltuv ends her book with a quote from Monique Wittig's Les Guérillères:

There was a time when you were not a slave, remember that. You walked alone, full of laughter, you bathed bare-bellied. You say you have lost all recollection of it, remember . . . you say there are no words to describe it, you say it does not exist. But remember. Make an effort to remember. Or, failing that, invent.

54

woman before Idea of woman

(for lilith)

Gayle Brandeis

Woman before Idea
of woman try to imagine...
woman before Idea
of high heels and high
breasts, before the concave
myth of belly, myth
of silence. woman
before Idea of woman—
body alive, every inch,
the cells shameless. sure;
true body of a woman.
woman before Idea
of woman. can you see
her? this is no "little
woman"—this woman fills
the rivers and bleeds deep
into the soil. woman before
Idea of woman. can you see
her dancing? she never stops
dancing, her bawdy body
streaming through the night.

55

The Story of Lilith and Hawwah

Savina J. Teubal

At the beginning of transformation, Lilith hovered over the Waters to calm them, so that she could call into being a resting place on dry Land, and find for herself a place of rest-(Isaiah 34:14). A New Moon appeared in the heavens, arousing the life-force as she swelled. And when the ground emerged she was arid; and so it was that Lilith formed the eden[1]—the steppe and the forest—and she called her Adamah.

Lilith gazed on her labor and sang:

> I rejoice in the Trees of the East,
> in the Plains of the West;
> with every shrub and blade
> My heart is filled.

The moon swelled to the First Quarter and Lilith ceased her work and rested; at her head, the Tree of Knowledge, at her feet, the Tree of Life.

As the Moon swelled to the Second Quarter, Lilith filled the waters with living things that swam; and in the sky she gave them wings:

And Lilith gazed on her labor and sang:

---

1. Sumerian, meaning "wilderness, steppe."

I rejoice in the Condor of the South,
the mighty Leviathan of the deep;
with every bird and fish
My heart is filled.

And Lilith called them by name: eagle and hummingbird, mackerel and conch; the Leviathan of the seas she named dolphin and whale.

Then Lilith called out: Adamah! Bring forth every kind of living thing. Lilith embraced Earth and breathed the breath of Life into her and Adamah brought forth every kind of living creature: creeping things, wild beasts and bees; animals of every kind.

Lilith gazed on her labor and sang:

I rejoice in the Bear of the north,
the Penguin of the south;
with the feline of the jungle
My heart is filled.

As the Moon swelled to the Third Quarter, Lilith said to all the living things: See, I give you every seed-bearing plant that is upon Earth, and every tree that has seed-bearing fruit; they shall be yours for food. To all the wild animals on land, to all the birds of the sky, and to everything that creeps on earth and swims in the waters in which there is breath of life, I give all the fruits and plants for food. And Lilith rested.

Yahweh of the gods[2] descended and gazed on the abundance of her labor and he ordered them: He planted all kinds of trees that were good for food and pleasing to look at, in the East around Lilith, so that her magical Trees stood in the middle of the Garden. And dark Lilith saw his paradise and praised it to Yahweh. Then Yahweh said to Lilith: The vegetation you conceived proliferates without order but my Garden must be cultivated; will you also generate life to tend to my Garden that it too may spring eternal?

As darkness fell, the Moon in her fullness appeared in the heavens and Lilith delivered Earthlings from the dust of the earth; female and male she conceived them.

---

2. The expression for deity used in Genesis 2 is Elohim (gods) or Yahweh-Elohim (Yahweh [of the] gods).

Lilith gazed on her labor and sang

I rejoice in all of my transformation,
in each creature I have made to live;
with everything that grows and breathes
My heart is filled.

Lilith smiled and made it a Holy Day. She called it Shabbatu[3] . . . because that day she ceased from her labors.

Yahweh of the gods filled his Garden with Lilith's living creatures: the cattle and the sheep to graze; the goats to climb and the ducks to swim. He set the Earthlings to till the Land and care for it. And Yahweh charged the Male, saying: From any tree of the Garden you must not eat of it, for it is fruit, the Fruit of divinity. For the day you eat of it you will die; you will be forced to leave the Garden and thus be severed from the Tree of Life.

One day, the female came to the magical Trees in the middle of the Garden and Lilith, in the guise of a serpent, asked her: Did the gods really say: You must not eat of any tree in the Garden? And the Female said to the Holy Serpent: We may eat of the fruit of the other trees in the Garden but only of the Fruit of the Tree in the middle of the Garden the gods say: You must not eat or touch it or you will die. And Lilith said to the Female: You will not die. The divine beings know that the day that you eat of my Tree of Knowledge your eyes will be opened and you will confer life like gods. You will render generations in your own image. But if you choose life you will also engender death: Without wisdom you cannot attain life or regeneration, you will remain virginal and live in the Garden forever but you will never know good from evil.

When the Female realized that the fruit of the Tree was nourishing and attractive because it was a source of wisdom, she took the fruit and ate. And her eyes were opened and she felt the blood gush from between her legs. In her wisdom, the Female gave some of the golden Fruit to her consort also, and he ate. Then their eyes were opened and they perceived the allure of their nakedness and clung to each other as one flesh. And the Female felt the spark of trans-

---

3. Akkadian, to desist. Ancient Babylonian Holy Day. Specifically "day of quieting of the heart."

formation in her belly and nourishment swell in her breasts.

And Lilith named the Female Hawwah (life) because she was the mother of all the living. The Male she named Adam (earth) for now he would return to Adamah from whence he was taken: for dust you are, and to dust you shall return.

Dark Lilith, pleased with her labors, spread her wings and flew back to her Cave by the Red Sea where she can be found to this day.

The Earthlings heard the sound of Yahweh of the gods moving about in the Garden at the breezy time of day; and Adam hid from Yahweh of the gods among the trees of the Garden. And Yahweh of the gods called out to Adam and said to him: Where are you? He replied, I heard the sound of you in the Garden, and I was afraid because I was naked, so I hid. Then he said: Who told you that you were naked? Did you eat from the Tree from which I had forbidden you to eat? And Adam said: Hawwah gave me of the Tree, and I ate.

And Yahweh of the gods said to Hawwah: What is this you have done! Hawwah answered: You forbade it only to Adam; you did not forbid it to me. The Holy Serpent offered me life and wisdom, and power over good and evil, and I took the Fruit and I ate. And when I knew that together we could conceive, I shared it with Adam, and he ate, and we rejoiced in the splendor of our nakedness.

And Yahweh of the gods said to himself: Now that they have become like one of us divine beings, what if they should stretch out their hand and take and eat also from the Tree of Life, mate and live forever!

Yahweh of the gods said to them: Because you did this, you must go out from my Garden for it can no longer contain you and the generations to come. You will abide in the wilderness (Eden), severed from the Tree of Life. Henceforth you yourselves must grow old and die, for you are now bearers of life.

So Yahweh of the gods closed the gates of his Garden. And Hawwah and Adam left Eden, to bring forth the generations to come.

Yahweh stationed East of the Garden the cherubim and the fiery every-turning sword, to guard the way to the Tree of Life.

56

Talking about Lilith

Layle Silbert

Hey, Yudl, I say, tell me about Lilith. Yudl is my confidant, my partner in conversation.

Lilith? I don't know anybody like that.
Right now you don't, I say. But before?
What're you talking about? Never did I have to do with people like that.
Like what? You're faking. Don't hide it. Don't be like the rest of them.
His turn to ask questions, also eyebrows. The rest of who?
What I mean is that after all you are a misogynist, I say. You just gave it away.
You're talking nonsense. I like women. In a way I can be said to love them.
All of us? I don't believe it. Even I don't love all men.
Me, too? He's worried. This could change his life. No more conversations?
Let's get to Lilith. Tell me.

Well, he draws the word out, looks up to the ceiling in a corner of the room. Following his gaze I see a few cobwebs. Who has cobwebs these days? No spiders.

Finally he speaks. It's true—he uses a faraway voice with a touch of tenderness. Her name was Lil, Lily—let me see, maybe Lilith like you say. I had to give her up. He sighs. What a beauty! Also a real live wire. Maybe too live. He lowers his head in grief. What a long time ago!

In that same faraway voice I say, So what happened?

They threw her out. They picked up their brooms, their dustrags, push her right through the doorway. They said, he's getting married. No room for you. Your kind we don't want.

Who said that?

You should know, he says.

What do you mean? They were wrong. A couple of poor misguided ladies. All of us want her back something terrible. Beautiful wild, lively Lilith. Come back.

Come back, Lilith, says Yudl.

We wait.

* * *

Hey, Yudl, I figured it out. Her name, before she changed it, was Gaia.

Ah, a nice name, he says. Who might that be?

The same as Lilith, remember her? Gaia was the real world, festooned in green such as nobody sees anymore.

What do you want me to do about that?

Right now, listen. So. One day comes somebody, a bad type, real capitalists, you know, wicked men, mean. They say, kick her out. We—they pound their chests—can make a better world for you.

And it wasn't so? says Yudl.

What they do is tear down the green, also they spit in the waters she drinks and bathes in, the way a waiter spits in soup once in a while. Then they kick her out. She's a witch, they say.

So? says Yudl.

Everybody listens to them, I go on. Anyway, did people have a choice? Who knows Gaia any more? In a few corners of the world maybe.

How can a round world have corners? says Yudl.

A good question, I say. Let's find her. We'll have to ask for Lilith. That's how we'll find Gaia, too. Let's go. A new world.

What do you mean? It's the old world, the love of my heart, says Yudl. Gaia, where are you? Lilith, oh, Lilith, come back.

57

Koan: What Is Your Relation to a Flower?

Norma Fain Pratt

Journal Notes

Mt. Althos Zen Center : Four-Day Meditation Program

Daily schedule

Morning
3:30 a.m.	Wake, chant
3:45	Tea, Meditation
4:30	Roshi-Koan
6:00	Meditation
7:00	Breakfast
7:30	Clean
8:00	Meditation
9:00–11:00	Work
11:00–12:45	Lunch and Rest

Afternoon
12:45–3:00	Meditation
3:15–5:00	Work
5:15–6:00	Dinner
6:00–7:30	Meditation, chanting
7:30–8:30	Roshi-Koan

8:35–9:00	Tea
9:00	Free

Thursday, January 28
9 p.m.

    There is a self in me. Living, speaking, confiding, guiding. I wonder what my koan, my question for study, will be tomorrow morning? The Roshi is walking toward the shower house; he appears cultivated. No one here is cynical. There is kindness and brusqueness as if everyone is existing, simply, in their skin. My hips ache, maybe from the high altitude. Having eaten the vegetarian food so fast is giving me gas. When I was a child, we still kept kosher and Mama took us to vegetarian restaurants. The same thing happened to me. So much goes the way I want it, these days. R. G. called last week. He says he still loves me and wants to be with me at the Retreat. He apologized for leaving me, hurting me that way two years ago. I said I accepted the apology. But, funny, my heart feels empty, numb as if I am incapable of loving anyone. To sleep now since 3:30 a.m. comes very early.

Day One
Friday, January 29
9:30 p.m.

    Wake before the morning bell. Alone in this dormitory room. As the only female I'm segregated. Pee in an earthen pot by taking off the acorn top. Sharp cold when I pull down my pants. A tiny bell at 3:30 a.m. and someone I can't see immediately turns on the light. Comb my hair, brush my teeth. Look out the door and I see the others are coming through the darkness. Can't tell one bald guy from another.

    Michael, the tall angular Australian in black monk's robes, explains the procedure. Bowing, kneeling, incense, "the whole bit," as he calls it. Before dawn the moon is still swimming. My first audience with the Roshi; he reminds me of the Japanese baby doll I bought years ago at an open market in Pasadena. Smooth, supple, round, soft-robed body, glittering eyes, humorous, waiting for a good joke. He asks in a heavy Japanese accent "You are not and you are? How do you realize this, without doubt?" I answer immediately: "Through trust. Trust renewed over and over again. A hard road to follow." He smiles, shakes his head almost as if he were shaking water from his nonexistent hair, and then he gives me my koan: "What is your relation to a flower? How do you realize the flower? The nature of the flower. The being a flower and not being a flower?" I think I answer: "By feeling its name because the flower has a presence when we name it." The Roshi's eyes glaze. "Continue working on this during meditation," he says.

The whole day's rituals delight me, but sitting in meditation hurts. I trust, I don't doubt.

> I'm like a flower to some people,
> an adornment.
> But to myself the flower cut and
> placed in a vase
> has lost its connection to
> the earth.
> The stalk soaks in water
> and has a hidden softness.

During the work period, I'm in the sewing room cutting collars for the monks' robes, and then Judy teaches me to use a Kenmore sewing machine. I stitch the same irregular lines I've made since Home Ec. class in elementary school. Sleep after lunch.

It looks like R. G. has decided not to come. At first I'm disappointed. What fun to have him sitting next to me in the Meditation hall. And the wickedness of it—a tryst in a Zen monastery. On second thought, not what I really want. I don't really believe in him. Now it starts to rain or snow. All sorts of disaster fantasies come to mind: snowed in at the top of this mountain without food with cannibals; car slides off icy cliff when trying to make it down. The light snow flakes on the granite are beautiful.

Day Two
Saturday, January 31 7:30 a.m.
The Roshi said the poem was too intellectual. Not Zen. I'm to understand the unity of nature, of God, of humans, of flowers. How is this realized? How am I related to the flower?

Day Three
Sunday, February 1 9 p.m.
Startled awake at 1:30 a.m. Frightened, thinking of death. I hear the door squeak open and a light comes into the room. At first it is

just a pinpoint frantically moving over the walls like a trapped little animal. Growing larger, it becomes human. An incandescent woman, with glowing burnt-buckwheat colored hair, huge yellow teeth, icy blue eyes, flowing along the wall, moaning in a rage. Seeking me out. Her rage is seeking me out. Coming closer and closer to me, she touches my hair. I jump out of bed. She is gone. The room is freezing cold. Stomach nausea, anxiety, caged. Was it a *makyo*, that thing the Zen people call an apparition, a mischievous evil spirit? Or the Lilith my mother once described by a quote from the Talmud: "Rabbi Hanina said: 'One may not sleep alone in a house, for whoever sleeps alone in a house is seized by Lilith.'" Maybe I'm drugged with sleep. Maybe the moving light, the noise, the apparition are only the automatic gas heater creaking to life. I fall back to sleep.

The bell rings at 3:30; lights turn on. Climb into my clothes. Pouring rain. Brush my teeth. Late to meditation. A kind monk gives me tea. Walk into meditation room. R. G. is sitting across from me in a full lotus position with his eyes wide open. I feel an electric shock. We meditate looking at one another. I notice the flowers to the right hand of the Buddha statue. Thinking, thinking of creation, mirroring, right-left hand. All creators and all created in the universe. The same essence as the flower.

Meeting with the Roshi I say: "I am a creator and a created." Boy, did the Roshi laugh. "No!" And he rings that little bell and waves me off.

I want vengeance. I want to move the goddamn flowers sitting in the vase at the Roshi's right side. But, I restrain myself. The Roshi will imagine I think I'm acting like God. So, no. What now? Make some more white collars.

Day Four February 2
Monday, 10:30 a.m.

The window panes in the Meditation Hall are dirty. Even Windex is not getting the hardened specks off the glass. The rituals and silent meals are exhausting me, freezing me. I play the same mental tapes from two years ago over and over: How R. G. betrays me. How I come to his house in Riverside, the door is locked. He's already left for Guatemala with his family. Without even a note. Next tape: Six months later. I come to his house in Riverside, again. He's there this time. He lets me in. Bachelor. Orderly. Ceramic pots. Macho Zen objects on the wall. He talks about his wife's death. "Even though she's gone, you and I have no future," he says. "What happened between us was the magic of that past moment." I'm ashamed.

Monday, 9:05 p.m.

The Roshi sits quietly, comfortably, passively, warm. Sandalwood incense exudes a pungent sweet smell. The Retreat is over tonight. This is my last chance to meet with him and answer my question. Suddenly, I cry. My heart is melting. Sobs. Big weightless tears run down my cheeks. A bowl of flowers is on the table. I take a dried, deep-brown buckwheat flower out and put it down in front of me. Standing up I run my fingers through my hair, holding my hair out like petals.

"Yes, he says, "that is so."

"Yes, I'm a flower," I say, flushing with embarrassment in front of a stranger, remembering Lilith's burned buckwheat hair and her anger.

I drop my hands. Myself, the flower disappears.

"Have I answered the koan?"

"No," he says, looking surprised by the question, "not yet," and he rings the bell for me to leave.

58

Lilith Sighted Starboard

Susan Gross

birth waters buoy
our gopher wood cocoon
reminding us
of the warm earth
yielding winter millet
and spring barley
we wives
run our hands along ark doorposts
stubbing our knuckles on mezzuzim
and ignore busy little noah
whose torso tosses seasick
and who punctures the air
with his staff
something tells us
he will have his millennium
for jabbing
after this forty-day hiatus
if we are lucky
we will land on a high mound
studded with the poplars of a sacred grove
where we will watch
unmoved
the erection of a tall tower and
rods cracking like whips

Lilith of the Wildwood, of the Fair Places

Susan Sherman

*And Lilith left Adam and went to seek her own place
And the gates were closed behind her and her name was
stricken from the Book of Life.*

1.
And how does one begin again

(Each time, each poem, each line, word, syllable
Each motion of the arms, the legs
a new beginning)

women women surround me
images of women their faces
I who for years pretended them away
pretended away their names their faces
myself what I am pretended it away
as a name exists to confine to define confine
define woman the name the word the definition
the meaning beyond the word the prism prison
beyond the word

to pretend it away

2.
It's the things we feel most
we never say for fear perhaps
that by saying them the things we care most
for will vanish
Love is most like that is the
unsaid thing behind the things we do
when we care most

3.
To be an outcast an outlaw
to stand apart from the Law the words
of the law
     outlaw
          outcast
cast out cast out by her own will
refusing anything but her own place
a place apart from any other
          her own
I do not have to read her legend in the ancient books
I do not have to read their lies
she is here inside me
I reach to touch her

my body my breath my life

4.
To fear you is to fear myself
To hate you is to hate myself
to desire you is to desire myself
to love you is to love myself

  Lilith of the Wildwood
  Lilith of the Fair Places

who eats her own children
who is cursed of God

Mother of us all

60
Lilith's Sabbath Prayer

Susan Gold

They remove your tiara
    with its Sabbath bells,
    the pendants from your breasts,
the velvet dress.
The story lies beneath your skirts.
They take care to unravel it,
your skin too sacred
to touch with bare hands.
How stripped you must feel,
Torah, Sabbath Bride lying naked,
thighs spread wide across the altar
while they sing the words of your cunt,
bless the womb of Man.

I want to join you there,
our skin wound together,
a goddess too powerful to touch.
I want to taste
your ancient song on my lips,
give birth to a new bride.

61

Achsah at the Spring

Helen Papell

Give me a blessing, for you have given me a south land; give me also springs of water.

—*Judges 1:15*

The spring my father gave me
weeps like Lilith's searching for her daughters.
Here, mothers scrub blood from battle clothes.
The water stumbles red.

We and the enemy
wait for bread.
Rain-birds fly past our fields.

Lilith, your daughters will return.
When my slave-mother was hungry
she didn't wait for a command,
she pulled the nipples of the Nile
to feed the desert.

We and the enemy wait for bread.
My husband gives me seeds
to grow warriors.

Lilith, your grief dribbles
down the other side of the hill
and is lost in the Jordan River.

Give me a blessing. Turn
toward my fields,
welcome the seeds I choose to plant
so the land may have peace.

VII

LILITH IN EXILE

Lilith became an important figure for Jews, as Aviva Cantor reminds us, in the period of Exile. This is ironic because she herself is often seen as in exile: the woman who left Eden to live alone by the Red Sea.

In this section, contemporary women respond to Lilith as a solitary figure, employing her as a means of expressing their own feelings of alienation from family and community. In one work, Lilith has many identities, but cannot "find . . . a real place" for herself. In another, she is the eternal outsider eternally persecuted as both woman and Jew. In others, she is growing older, facing menopause and her own mortality. (Kabbalists believe Lilith will die when the Messiah comes.) Aging and wounded, she, like other women, questions her earlier choices. Finally, she is depicted as a suicide who paradoxically continues living, reflecting on the cycles of life and death.

62
Lilith, in This Dream
Leah Schweitzer

1.
I have thousands of names   in this dream
trickster   shadowy flamewoman
angry child-woman   fiery night-woman
and, in the dream   I try to take on
the form of a human   can't seem to find
a real place   for myself

2.
With Adam   I always end up on the bottom
ask why   complain   get no answers
I fly off angry   outraged   and
as I escape   I dare to pronounce
God's ineffable name   spew curses
but I can't seem to find a real place for myself

3.
I fear amulets   won't get near them
they take my strength away
                        I terrorize
women in childbirth   try to strangle
their newborn   send wet-dreams
down the loins of men
the angels warn me: my children
will be demons   in this dream
and I can't seem to find a   place for myself

4.
Now I live in exile   move from cave to cave
the air   too thin to breathe
I fly the world at night   in ragged wings
    my flaming hair turned white   and wiry
I hover   I watch   I lurk in shadows
insist on hanging around   forever
I live out my destiny

63
Drawn to the Flames
Nina Judith Katz

It has begun to matter very little whether they kill me as woman or as Jew. When I go back to Medieval Europe, I now wear pants. Sometimes that is the offense for which they kill me. Sometimes other Jews stone me. Occasionally even other women attack me. Usually, of course, I am sentenced to the stake by the white Christian men masterminding the Inquisition.

I have taken to wearing fringe and a *kippah*,[1] and have grown my hair long again as a sign that I have no wish to look like a man. I wear my hair in one long braid down my back, out of my way, and I only need to rebraid it once a week or so. When I fly, both broomstick and braid veer straight out behind me. But I tuck in my braid and don an oversized black jacket and top hat when I go to the men's Kaballah circles. And I tuck my fringe in when I give my under-the-underground women's Kabballah workshops. But when I go outside I wear my braid and fringe out with pride; for I am willing to hide in the name of learning, be I student or teacher, but not for the sake of mere safety, so precarious even with all precautions.

The schizophrenia is in the century hopping. When I come back to the twentieth century, twentieth-century doubt and preoccupa-

---

1. Hebrew; a yarmulke, or skullcap traditionally worn by observant Jewish men although women are not forbidden to wear it.

tion come back to me. So, in the twentieth century I wear my *kippah* only at prayer times, and only at those prayer times which doubt and preoccupation release me to observe. I wear my *tallith katan*[2] sporadically, letting it serve as a day-long reminder of my a.m. mood. And I keep my fringe tucked in when I'm among the neighboring gentiles, as they no longer know what it means. I let down my fringe among intimates only.

Hair and attire no longer distinguish men from women. If long hair on a woman signifies anything, men misread it as a sign of vulnerability, which oddly fails to remind them of Samson. So I wear my hair short and study martial arts. Inducing the all-nothingness of the state of sweat, they go well with mysticism.

I don't know which continent or century is less my home. I feel drawn to the flames. Their jumping orange heat entrances me as surely as the Voice. Perhaps that is why I still go back to Medieval Europe, even though I survive in twentieth-century America rather more often.

---

2. Hebrew, an undershirt worn to remind the observant Jew of the 613 *mitzvot* (commandments) represented by as many fringes on the corners of the shirt. The commandment to wear this is said to apply only to men, although women are not forbidden to wear it.

Lilith, I Don't Cut My Grass

Enid Dame

Lilith, I don't cut my grass
 as you never cut your hair.
I picture you in my backyard
where it's always cool and ferny,
where jewelweeds grow taller than trees,
where wild berries tangle
like knots in cats' fur.

I see you sorting out the birds from the cats:
two of your favorite animals.
Contradictions never scared you.

Lilith, you smell like the earth
and marigolds and mulchy leaves.
Your arms are mud-bespattered.
You don't look like my mother.

I couldn't ask my mother
for a blessing.
She was too much afraid
of her own craziness.
She only spoke to cats.

Every few months
She went to an expert
to burn all the wilderness
out of her hair.

Once she tried to take me with her.
I scratched and fought,
yowled, ran up an elm tree.
It took years to climb down.

Lilith, I'm almost 50.
I'm running out of time, money, eyesight.
I still bleed   but for how long?

Not like this yard where everything is liquid:
where roses sag and break their waters,
tomatoes offer up their juices,
slugs die dreamily in beerbowls,
you dip your toes in green mud.

Lilith, neighbors are complaining.
They're collecting money
to buy me a power mower.
How can I tell them
I'm terrified of power?
There's too much let loose in the world.
It's one gift I don't need.

Lilith, it's growing later
I know you won't hang on forever.
They say Messiah's coming any day now.
I hear his footsteps ringing in the hallway.
The clean clang of authority.
I see his shadow looming
big as a condominium
sucking up the sun.

No stopping that man!
He's carrying a squirtgun filled with chemicals.
No room for weeds in his world.

Lilith, bless this garden
while both of us
still use it.

65
Lilith, Wounded
F. Dianne Harris

Hidden amongst branches of a wild fig tree,
Lilith knows the clocks no longer stop.
Her sexuality dormant beneath a shimmering,
slipping shawl, she grows older.
Today's rain cannot moisten her parched tear ducts.
Sorrow lies proud in her stone-dead heart.
Blood has ceased to spill from her loins
but beats furiously in her temples,
flushes her cheeks with dry-eyed shame.
Feathers float from her molting wings,
mix with dried, curled leaves
at her taloned feet.

When the white owl shrieks and glares,
yellow-eyed, at passersby, she doesn't flinch
but pulls leonine locks close beneath her chin,
gazes steadily at the serpent whose
offering she once denied,
wonders how it might have been
to lie beneath the ribs of Adam
rather than roam the night skies forever
with unquenched, unabated fervor,
lover after lover.
She remains outside, forever.
Lilith, wounded.

66

The Last Lilith Poem

Lynne Savitt

Sunday she called
 her mother, ex-husband,
 several friends, her lover
to tell them she was leaving
her two small children
alone she was going
to a salt blue world
a banquet of seaweed draped on their necks

Inside Lilith's head was a conch
which sent poems to her fingers
She placed her ear to the sea green paper to hear the ocean

Her closet was half empty
her shawls and dictionary were gone

Her mother said she was overly dramatic
Her ex-husband said she was trying to seduce the N.Y. Times
Her lover sighed with a stewardess and relief
the bay applauded her

Summers, strange unexplainable cramps
attack swimmers who sink smiling
A few winter fishermen never returned
from their mornings robbing water

If you listen to the pink
breasted shells you can
hear her whisper,
"Everything is posthumous."

Afterword: Lilith Lives

Lilly Rivlin

Lilith is hot! Known for her multifaceted permutations throughout the centuries Lilith has emerged from her Exile, this time in the guise of a high-powered group of female musicians touring under the name of *Lilith Fair*. In the summer of 1997, *Lilith Fair*, a showcase of female songwriters, organized by Canadian songwriter Sarah McLachlan, launched a thirty-two-city tour with a sold-out show in a 20,000-seat natural amphitheater in the town of George, in Washington State, 150 miles east of Seattle. Ms. McLachlan called Lilith "the world's first feminist." The *Lilith Fair* tour features sixty-one women and their bands—among them Sheryl Crow, Joan Osborne, Mary Chapin Carpenter, Lisa Loeb, Emmylou Harris, Tracy Chapman, and the Indigo Girls. Lilith was relegated for centuries to the demimonde of demons and witches; now, as the icon of *Lilith Fair*, her tale is told on *Good Morning America*, the *New York Times*, cover stories in *Time* and *Entertainment Weekly*, and other publications. The performers say Lilith provides positive role models for their largely young and female audience. In her ode to the fair, singer/poet Kinnie Starr bellowed, "Lilith was banned from the garden of man, but she's back in our face!"

- In Los Angeles, graffiti scrawled on the side of an underpass wall reads "Lilith Lives."
- In Tel Aviv, a popular restaurant bears the name of Lilith.
- A female rock group calling themselves the Bohemian Women's Political Alliance claims Lilith as one of their heroes.
- In 1998, filmmaker Lynne Sachs released "A Biography of Lilith" a short film depicting her version of Lilith.
- Early in 1997 *Lilith*, a Jewish women's magazine, celebrated twenty years in existence, and is still going strong.
- In the fall of 1997, "Lilith," an abstract show of contemporary paintings featuring six New York Jewish artists, opened in The Work Space, an exhibition space in Soho. The artists, all women, approached Lilith each in her own way, but all embody her spirt of risk taking and evoke deep emotions. Artists: Andrea Belag, Cora Cohn, Harriet Korman, Louise Fishman, Melissa Meyer, Joan Snyder.
- In the same year, in New York City, Deborah Drattell composed an opera called *Lilith*.
- In the summer of 1995, *Adam and Lilith and Eve*, an opera by John Bramhall, premiered in Maine
- In 1995, Serpentine, an innovative composer/performer of women-centered vocals and music, recorded her third CD/tape on Goddess Rock Records. It included the haunting song "Lilith" as well "Innana," another undomesticated lady.
- In 1993, Mari Anne Franzese, trying to decide on a name for her daughter while in labor, heard her husband, Lee Chasen, say, "Let's call her Lilith." The demonology associated with the name scared Mari Anne, but "when I read about Lilith as a Wind Spirit, that brought more balance. When I looked at my daughter's serene face, I thought, 'Welcome home. There was no reason for you to be cast out.' There was a look of recognition on her face, like the lightness of being."
- In the same year, Liz Lauren Leviton, of Baltimore, Maryland, began her Bat Mitzvah speech with the story of Lilith. "I told my rabbi I wanted to speak about Judaism, feminism, women in the Bible and tie it all to my family. He suggested Lilith," she said.
- In 1991, David Schechter wrote and Margot Stein Azen created the music and lyrics to a "new musical myth," *Guarding the Garden*, a light-hearted, environmentally sensitive play featuring Adam, Eve, and Lilith.
- In 1973, sculptor and mask maker Suzanne Benton created a Lilith mask and gave her first of many performances of Lilith's story as part of her series "Ritual Tales of Women of Myth and Heritage." She is still performing.

Afterword: Lilith Lives

Lilith has come a long way since my article appeared in *Ms.* magazine in December 1972. Though the *Ms.* editors I worked with were pleased to publish an article about Adam's first wife, few had heard of her. Sources were scant, mostly arcane, or works of academics writing about mythology—all male (Raphael Patai, Louis Ginzberg, Joseph Campbell).

Throughout history, an archetype representing "the nondomesticated woman [who] exemplifies all the fear and attraction that such a woman elicits," has existed. "She is the exception to the rule, the woman who does not behave in societally approved ways, the goddess who models the crossing of gender lines and the danger that this presents."[1] As the freewheeling Sumerian goddess Inanna (a.k.a. Ishtar, Isis) or as Lilith, Adam's first wife of Jewish legends, who flew off to exile on the Red Sea rather than remain with a controlling husband, or as the object of a nineteenth-century-poet's sexual imagination, this archetype has always been a male creation, transforming and transmuting according to the prevailing moral strictures and morals of the times.

Myth and fantasies evolve as a reaction to prevailing societal pressures and change. In Victorian England, as women demanded their rights, Dante Gabriel Rossetti wrote and painted a mythic "Lady Lilith" as an alluring if not dangerous sex object. Her veil of hair attracts, seduces, and finally strangles the victim of her charm. In her book *The Soul of Lilith*, Marie Corelli, a nineteenth-century romantic writer, tells the story of El Rami, a scientist, who brings a beautiful, but dead, woman named Lilith back to life and falls passionately in love with her. The story is characteristic of the Victorian preoccupation with the conflict among reason (science) and love, art, and soul.

In the highly regulated if not constrained societies of Europe and the Middle East, few alternatives to the virtuous mother/wife role for woman existed. Natural, but denied, impulses were relegated to the underworld of witchcraft, dark demonic stereotypes. In some parts of Europe, the myth of the Black Virgin satisfied women's need for a dark archetype.

In the latter part of the twentieth century, self-sufficient women,

---

1. Tikva Frymer-Kensky, *In the Wake of the Goddess: Women, Culture and the Biblical Transformation of Pagan Myth* (New York: Fawcett Columbine, published by Ballantine Books, 1993), p. 25.

inspired by the women's movement, have adopted the Lilith myth as their own. They have transformed her into a female symbol for autonomy, sexual choice, and control of one's own destiny.

With women in some positions of power, our myths and fantasies were bound to change. Since "Lilith" appeared in *Ms.* more than two decades ago there has been a creative burst of works—Midrash, books (biblical studies, Jungian analysis, literature, psychodrama), articles, songs, dances, operas—featuring Lilith in the title role. The stories, essays, poems, and midrashim in this anthology surely illustrate what happens to Lilith when she comes out of women's experience rather than from a man's head.

Although this volume is a selection of Jewish women's writings on Lilith, it is essential to state that Jewish men and non-Jewish men and women have also written about her since she has emerged as a feminist icon.

As John Mendelsohn wrote in his review of the "Lilith" abstract painting exhibition:

> Lilith has made it all the way back from pariah to icon. With all the force of the return of the repressed she has entered the feminist pantheon, as goddess, exemplar of female strength, passionate and natural, keeper of dark mysteries. As the literature on Lilith grows, her name appears with increasing frequency in a wide variety of cultural settings.[2]

Why has Lilith finally taken off? Even the Second Wave of the Women's Movement did not attend to our sensual and sexual impulses. Certainly, there were Nancy Friday and Erica Jong. Betty Dodson painted her clitoris canvases and gave workshops on how to have the cosmic orgasm, but really only in the last decade have a large number of women expressed their sensual and sexual power; for example, *Lilith Fair*, and Naomi Wolf in *Promiscuities*. To paraphrase Lacan, it is only when we women imagine ourselves as subjects that we can be free of masculine paradigms.

The women's movement has made us conscious that the personal is political. My own experience as a girl, and as a woman, in pre-1960s America led me to Lilith. (Until then the only role models I

---

2. John Mendelsohn, "The Abstract Lilith," *The Jewish Week*, New York, August 29, 1997.

could relate to were two comic-strip heroes: Brenda Starr, girl reporter, and Wonder Woman). The specific attributes I latched on to, even before a coherent sense of Lilith had emerged in me, were her independence and need for freedom, her sensuality and sexuality. I felt alone though clearly I was not. And then came the feminist movement. How wonderful it felt as someone who was once told by a Freudian psychoanalyist that I had a character disorder because I identified with Lilith. And how amazing it feels now that millions of women have this "same" character disorder of needing to celebrate freedom, exuberance, sensuality.

When men created the myth of Lilith, she was a stereotype. She remained a man's fantasy. Not long ago a male friend, responding to a feminist reaction I had to his macho remark, said, "You have to accept your order in this universe." He meant that my gender determined my place in the universe. Lacan suggests gender is a construct and belongs in the realm of "masquerade" (both masculine and feminine).[3] This term was originally coined by lay analyst Joan Rivière, for whom it was symptomatic of a failed femininity.[4] When my friend said I had to accept my order—my place essentially—in this universe, I understood, once more, how all women have been objectified over these many generations. And that is the critical difference. Women are no longer accepting being defined and objectified by men. That is why Lilith lives today in all her multifarious manifestations.

---

3. *Feminine Sexuality—Jacques Lacan and the école freudienne*, ed. Juliet Mitchell and Jacqueline Rose, trans. Jacqueline Rose (New York and London: Pantheon Books and W. W. Norton, 1982), p. 43
4. Joan Rivière, "Womanliness as Mascarade," *IJPA* 10, (1929).

Contributors

Elaine Rose Barnartt-Goldstein was born in Pittsburgh, Pennsylvania, and discovered feminism and traditional Judaism at Indiana University. She learned of Lilith from *Lilith* magazine's first issue and has hardly missed one since. After graduating Brandeis and Northeastern, she has been working as a speech-language pathologist in Boston, Massachusetts.

Gayle Brandeis's work has appeared in such publications as *Mosaic, Mothering,* and *The Infant's Cry,* as well as the anthology *Eating Our Hearts Out.* Awards include a PEN American Center Grant and a Poetry in Motion Award. She lives in Riverside, California, with her husband, Matt McGunigle, and their children, Arin and Hannah.

Sue D. Burton is a physician's assistant working in women's health care in Vermont. Her poetry has appeared in *Calyx, Sinister Wisdom,* and *West Branch* and in *Onion River: Six Vermont Poets* (R.N.M., 1997). Her interview with poet James McMichael is forthcoming in *Agni.*

Aviva Cantor, a journalist and lecturer, is the author of *Jewish Women, Jewish Men: The Legacy of Patriarchy in Jewish Life*, a feminist interpretation of Jewish history (HarperCollins, 1995). She co-founded *Lilith* magazine and authored *The Egalitarian Hagada* (Beruriah Books) and compiled/edited the *Bibliography on the Jewish Woman, 1900-1985* (Biblio Press).

Ilona Chessid (translator) was born in New York in 1960. She has a Ph.D. in Romance Languages and Literatures, and has published articles on French literature, as well as a book on the novels of Emile Zola.

Enid Dame's books of poetry include *Anything You Don't See* (West End), *Miriam's Water*, and *Lilith and Her Demons* (Cross-Cultural Communications). Her midrashic poems have appeared in *New York Quarterly*, *Tikkun*, and *Many Mountains Moving*. She teaches at New Jersey Institute of Technology and co-edits *Home Planet News* with her husband, Donald Lev.

Shoshana T. Daniel lives in Eugene, Oregon, where she is a counselor in private practice. Her work has appeared in numerous publications, including *fiction international*, *QUIX*, *Northeast Journal*, *Sojourner*, *Calliope*, *In The Family*, and the anthology *Every Woman I've Ever Loved: Lesbian Writers on Their Mothers* (Reid/Iglesias, Eds.).

Sandy Bodek Falk is training to be an obstetrician and gynecologist. She continues to write and to be inspired by her family tree—her rich collection of holocaust survivors, Israeli freedom fighters, and hasidic *rebbetzin* and rabbis.

Henri Cohen Solal, born in Paris, has lived in Jerusalem since 1980. Educator, psychotherapist, and analyst, he has conducted seminars on psychoanalysis and Judaism since 1976. Currently completing a dissertation on Freud's Jewish identity, he and Danielle Storper Perez lead a study group on texts of Jewish tradition and work together on feminine biblical texts.

Ruth Feldman has five books of poetry and fourteen of Italian translations to her credit, all poetry except for Primo Levi's concentration camp stories. She has read at numerous universities here and in Italy. Major awards: John Florio, Circe-Sabaudia, the Italo Calvino, and an NEA literary translators' fellowship. She is the only American in the Primo Levi documentary film.

Elaine Frankonis works at Cultural and Arts Resources, New York State Education Department. Publications: *Albany Tricentennial Literary Anthology: Gates to the City, Washout, Indigo, Tin Wreath,* and *The Berkshire Review*. She lives outside Albany, and spends most of her spare time ballroom dancing and communicating with her kids over the Internet.

Naomi Gal, a veteran Israeli writer, worked in Israeli television and the newspapers *Ma'Ariv* and *Yediot Ahronot*. Author of eight books, her novel *Soap Opera* won the Jerusalem prize and was on Israel's best seller list. *Lilith*, her new novel, is published by Keter. Gal was born in Jerusalem and is going to die there.

Mary L. Gendler, psychologist, photographer, world traveler, and feminist, has written on Jewish feminist subjects since 1970. Her article about Lilith appeared in *Jewish Heritage* twenty-five years ago. Her work with children of divorce stimulated the story in this anthology. Married for thirty-four years, she has two married daughters and a grandson.

Susan Gold found Lilith to be a rich source of inspiration while writing poetry for her master's thesis at San Diego State University. She currently lives in the San Francisco Bay Area and is writing her first novel, which explores contemporary Jewish themes.

Naomi Goodman, peace activist and historian, is working on her book about Eve and Lilith. She is co-author of *The Goodbook Cookbook;* co-editor of *The Challenge of Shalom: The Jewish Tradition of Peace and Justice*; past president of The Jewish Peace Fellowship; mother and grandmother.

Ona Gritz-Gilbert has an M.A. from the writing program at New York University. Her poetry has appeared in *The American Voice, Poetry East, Heresies,* and *Home Planet News*. She is the author of *Starfish Summer*, a novel for children (HarperCollins, 1998).

Susan Gross is a freelance writer specializing in feminist Midrash and Jewish archives. Her work has appeared in *Lilith, Taking the Fruit, Reading Between the Lines,* and *Biblical Women in the Midrash.* She lives in Shreveport, Los Angeles, with her husband and two daughters.

F. Dianne Harris, a founding member of Women in the Visual and Literary Arts, divides her time between Houston and northern New Mexico. A recipient of various awards from the Houston chapter of the Texas Society of Poetry, her work appears in *The Ledge, Borderlands, Insomnia, El Locofoco, Poetry Motel,* and other publications.

Grace Herman's poetry has been published in such periodicals as *The Minnesota Review, The Colorado Quarterly, Jewish Frontier, Embers, and Poetpourri,* among others. A retired physician, her first book of poems, *Set Against Darkness,* was published by The National Council of Jewish Women, New York Section, in 1992.

Barbara D. Holender of Buffalo, New York, is the author of *Shiva Poems: Poems of Mourning* (1989), *Ladies of Genesis* (1991), *Is This The Way To Athens?* (1996), and a children's book in Hebrew, *Ani Cli-zemer* (1996). Her poems have appeared in numerous journals and anthologies. She is a recipient of the Hans S. Bodenheimer Award for Poetry.

Naomi Mara Hyman is the editor of *Biblical Women in the Midrash,* a poet, midrashist, teacher of Jewish women's spirituality, board member of the Institute of Contemporary Midrash; holds a master's degree in Jewish Studies and is pursuing rabbinic ordination. Her work has appeared in *Kerem: Creative Explorations in Judaism.*

Louise Jaffe, Professor Emerita of English at Kingsborough Community College and poetry editor for the New Press Literary Quarterly, has recently published her fourth poetry collection, *The Great Horned Owl's Proclamation and Other Hoots.* Her poems have appeared in *Sarah's Daughters Sing* and *The Jewish Women's Literary Annual.*

Nina Judith Katz is a poet, fiction writer, lexicographer, translator, technical writer, and editor. She has recently completed her first novel, *The Repatriots*. She lives in Somerville, Massachusetts.

Elana Klugman, psychotherapist, writer, and mother of 9-year-old Noah and 5-year-old Sara, lives in western Massachusetts with her husband Jeff. She has published poems in *The New Our Bodies, Ourselves* by the Boston Women's Health Book Collective, *Mothering* magazine, and *Peregrine*.

Barbara Black Koltuv, Ph.D., is a clinical psychologist and Jungian analyst in private practice in Manhattan. In addition to *The Book of Lilith*, she has written *Weaving Woman* and *Solomon and Sheba* (Nicolas-Hays). She explores the transformative and individuating aspects of love and sexuality. She is currently writing *Dreams of Love/The Song of Songs*.

Jacqueline Lapidus, a veteran of international feminist groups, is an editor, teacher, and theologian. Her poems and essays have appeared in numerous publications; her books include *Ready to Survive, Starting Over, Ultimate Conspiracy*, and an unpublished collection tentatively entitled *Cape & Islands*. She lives in Provincetown and Boston.

Jo Milgrom is author of two books: *The Akedah: The Binding of Isaac, a Primary Symbol in Jewish Thought and Art* and *Handmade Midrash: Exercises in Visual Theology*. She is an assemblage sculptor and poet, currently living and teaching in Jerusalem with her husband, Jacob Milgrom.

Rochelle Natt reviews poetry for *American Book Review* and *ACM*. She has published poetry in *Iowa Review, California Quarterly, Negative Capability, The MacGuffin, Fresh Ground, Mudfish, Chachalaca Poetry Review*, and in many anthologies such as *More Golden Apples* (Papier Mache Press) and *With a Whale's Wit, Fly's Eye* (Cleis Press).

Haviva Ner-David, 28, a Ph.D. candidate at Bar-Ilan University, and a student and teacher of Torah, writes both fiction and nonfiction. An activist on behalf of feminism and religious pluralism in Israel and the Diaspora, she is a self-declared religious feminist. Haviva lives in Jerusalem with her husband and two young children.

Lesléa Newman is an author and editor who has twenty-five titles to her credit, including many books with Jewish themes such as *Matzo Ball Moon* and *Remember That* (children's books); *In Every Laugh a Tear* (novel); *Fat Chance* (young adult novel); and *A Letter to Harvey Milk* (short story collection).

Alicia Ostriker has published eight books of poetry. *The Crack in Everything* (1996) was a National Book Award finalist, and won the Paterson Poetry Prize. She is also the author of *The Nakedness of the Fathers*, which combines Midrash and autobiography.

Helen Papell, librarian, storyteller, puppeteer, and poet of feminist Midrash, has published *Talking with Eve Leah Hagar Miriam*. Anthology and journal publications include *Downtown, Jewish Women's Literary Annual, Negative Capability, Outerbridge, Prairie Schooner, Sarah's Daughters Sing,* and *Verve*. She was a Pushcart Prize nominee.

Alix Pirani is a psychotherapist and writer based in Great Britain. Working within the traditions of humanistic and transpersonal psychology, she runs workshops in dynamic mythology and spirituality. She is the author of *The Absent Father: Crisis and Creativity* and the editor of *The Absent Mother: Restoring the Goddess to Judaism and Christianity*.

Judith Plaskow, professor of religious studies at Manhattan College, writes and lectures widely on feminist theology. She is author of *Standing Again at Sinai: Judaism from a Feminist Perspective*.

Norma Fain Pratt, Ph.D., teaches the history of women and writes scholarly and fictional works. Her articles about Yiddish women writers include the pioneering "Culture and Radical Politics: Yiddish Women Writers, 1880–1940," in *American Jewish History*. Her stories have been published in *Lilith* and *Studies in American Jewish Literature*.

Mindy Rinkewich, born in New York City, where she lives and works as a legal interpreter, is the author of a collection of poems, *The White Beyond the Forest* (Cross-Cultural Communications). A second collection, *The Sweet Kid from Warsaw* (Jewish Women's Resource Center), is forthcoming. She is a translator of Yiddish, Russian, and Polish poetry.

Lilly Rivlin, a seventh-generation Jerusalemite, is a writer/filmmaker and feminist activist living in Manhattan. She has published in the *The Washington Post, Newsweek, Ms., Lilith, Noga*, conceived and photographed *When Will the Fighting Stop? A Child's View of Jerusalem* (Atheneum, 1990), and researched *O Jerusalem* by Larry Collins and Dominique LaPierre.

Lynn Saul practices law in Tucson, Arizona, and teaches poetry and composition at Pima College. Her poems have appeared in magazines and anthologies including *Sarah's Daughters Sing*, the *Jewish Women's Literary Annual, Crossing Limits*, and *SandScript*. A finalist in the Hans Bodenheimer Jewish poetry series, she has won the Flagstaff Festival of the Arts poetry award.

Lynne Savitt is the author of six books of poetry. Her latest is *Sleeping Retrospect of Desire* (Konocti Books, 1993).

Jane Schapiro is the author of a book of poetry, *Tapping This Stone* (Washington Writers' Publishing House). Her work has appeared in *The American Scholar, The Gettysburg Review, Prairie Schooner*, and *Yankee* among other places. She lives in northern Virginia with her husband and three daughters.

Joanne Seltzer's poems have appeared widely in anthologies, such as *When I Am an Old Woman I Shall Wear Purple*, and in literary journals such as *Alchemy* and *Painted Bride Quarterly*. She has also published short fiction, literary essays, translations of French poetry, and three poetry chapbooks.

Suzy Shabetai, British born, has lived in Jerusalem since 1968. She is a major translator of Israeli writers, among whom are Yeshua Bar Yosef, Batya Gur, and Dan Pagis.

Susan Sherman, poet, playwright, editor of *Ikon* magazine, has published three collections of poetry; a translation, *Shango de Ima* (Doubleday, 1971); and *Color of the Heart: Writing from Struggle & Change, 1959–1990* (Curbstone, 1990.) Awards: 1997 NYFA fellowship (Creative Nonfiction Literature), 1990 NYFA fellowship (Poetry), Puffin Grant (1992).

Layle Silbert, writer and photographer, recently published her third book of stories, *New York, New York,* with St. Andrews Press. She has published numerous stories and poems in various magazines and a handful of anthologies.

Frieda Singer, an honored creative writing teacher, has published in *The Formalist, The South Florida Poetry Review, Negative Capability,* and the anthology *Blood to Remember: American Poets on the Holocaust.* She is an award recipient from the Poetry Society of America, Pen and Brush, and The World Order of Narrative and Formalist Poets.

Judith Skillman's books are *Worship of the Visible Spectrum* (Breitenbush, 1988) and *Beethoven and the Birds,* (Blue Begonia Press, 1996). Her poems have appeared in *Northwest Review, Southern Review, Iowa Review, Poetry, Yellow Silk,* and other journals. In 1991 she was awarded a Washington State Arts Commission Writer's Fellowship.

Julia Stein has published two books of poetry: *Under the Ladder to Heaven* and *Desert Soldiers.* She writes about women's and working-class literature. Her essay "Industrial Music: Contemporary American Working Class Poetry and Modernism" appeared in the Working Class Studies Issue of *Women's Studies Quarterly* (June 1995). She won a Puffin Grant in 1997.

Nikki Stiller, author of *Notes of a Jewish Nun* (Cross-Cultural Communications, 1992), has published work in *Primavera, Midstream, Home Planet News,* and *The New York Times Book Review.* Associate professor at New Jersey Institute of Technology, she cares for her mother, Blanche, 88, and son, Jean-Paul, 4, while working on a new book of poems.

Danielle Storper Perez, French born, living in Jerusalem since 1978, is an anthropologist and researcher at the National Center for French Scientific Research. Published in various sociological works on contemporary Israel and the anthropology of Judaism, she is a co-founder of a branch of the women's liberation movement in France and a peace activist in Israel.

Savina J. Teubal lectures and writes extensively on women in the Hebrew Bible. Author of *Sarah the Priestess: The First Matriarch of Genesis* (1984) and *Ancient Sisterhood: The Lost Traditions of Hagar and Sarah* (Ohio University Press, 1997), she is a founding president of *Sarah's Tent: Sheltering Creative Jewish Spirituality*, a Southern California-based organization.

Henny Wenkart, Ph.D., Philosophy, Harvard, and M.S., Journalism, Columbia, is editor of *Sarah's Daughters Sing* and the *Jewish Women's Literary Annual*. Translator of Pauline Wengeroff's *Memoirs*, she is writing a philosophical novel and a poetry cycle, *The Philanderer's Wife*. She is married and has three married children and a number of grandchildren.

Ruth Whitman is author of eight books of poetry and three of translation. Award and fellowships include: Senior Fulbright Writer-in-Residence, Hebrew University; NEA; Radcliffe College, Bunting Institute; Rhode Island State Council on the Arts; Alice Fay di Castongnola, Poetry Society of America; Guinness International Poetry; Kovner, Jewish Book Council of America.

Naomi Wolf lives in New York City. Her books *The Beauty Myth* and *Fire with Fire* were international bestsellers as is her latest work, *Promiscuities*. The first two books were *New York Times* Notable Books of the Year. *The New York Times* called *The Beauty Myth* one of the seventy most significant books of the century.

Credits

Sara Eve Baker. "Lilith and the Gang" is used by permission of the author.

Elaine Rose Barnartt-Goldstein. "A Midrash on the Creation of Woman" is used by permission of the author.

Gayle Brandeis. "woman before the Idea of woman" is used by permission of the author.

Sue D. Burton. "Lilith at the Red Sea" is used by permission of the author.

Aviva Cantor. "Lilith, the Woman Who Would Be A Jew" is reprinted from *Jewish Women, Jewish Men: the Legacy of Patriarch in Jewish Life*. HarperCollins, © 1995 by Aviva Cantor. Reprinted by permission of the author.

Enid Dame. "Lilith" is reprinted from *Lilith and Her Demons* (Cross-Cultural Communications, 1986). Reprinted by permission of the author. © 1986 by Enid Dame. "Lilith, I Don't Cut My Grass," *American Voice* 32 (Fall 1994), reprinted by permission of the author. "Sister in the Shadows: Lilith's Role in the Jewish Family Myth" will appear, in different form, in *Phoebe: An Interdisciplinary Feminist Journal*. Printed with permission of the author.

Shoshana T. Daniel. "Sonnet for a Jewish Woman" is reprinted from *Brown Journal of the Arts*. Reprinted by permission of the author. "Ghazals for a Demon Daughter" appears in a libretto of *Songs for the Daughters of Lilith*, Will Ayton, composer, and is used with permission of the author. "If There Were Angels" is used by permission of the author.

Sandy Bodek Falk. "Lilith" is used by permission of the author.

Ruth Feldman. "Riding the Wind's Wing" appeared under the title "Lilith" in *The Ambition of Ghosts* (Green River Press, 1979). © 1979 by Ruth Feldman. Reprinted by permission of the author.

Elaine Frankonis. "Lilith Returns" is used by permission of the author.

Naomi Gal. "Lilith's Divorce" is used by permission of the author.

Mary L. Gendler. "The First Divorce" is used by permission of the author.

Susan Gold. "In the Garden" is reprinted from *Bridges, a Journal for Jewish Feminists and Our Friends*, vol. 5, no. 1 (June 1995). Reprinted by permission of the author. "Lilith's Sabbath Prayer," and "Divine Mornings" are used by permission of the author.

Naomi Goodman. "Lilith and Eve: Secret Sisters and Successive Wives" is an excerpt from a work in progress, used by permission of the author.

Ona Gritz-Gilbert. "Lilith's Version" is used by permission of the author.

Susan Gross. "Lilith Sighted Starboard" is used by permission of the author.

F. Dianne Harris. "Chameleon" is reprinted from *Bayousphere*, 1993. Reprinted by permission of the author. "Lilith Wounded" is reprinted from *Arrowsmith* and is used by permission of the author.

Grace Herman. "Adam" is used by permission of the author.

Barbara D. Holender. "Drifting Like Smoke" first appeared under the title "Lilith" in *Ladies of Genesis* (Jewish Women's Resource Center). © 1991 by Barbara D. Holender. Reprinted by permission of the author.

Naomi Mara Hyman. "Lilith's Loophole" appeared in a modified version as "Lilith" in *Kerem* (Winter 1994). It is used by permission of the author.

Louise Jaffe. "Sisters" is used by permission of the author.

Nina Judith Katz. "Drawn to the Flames" is used by permission of the author.

Elana Klugman. "Guilt and Knitting" is used by permission of the author.

Barbara Black Koltuv. "The Book of Lilith: A Summary" is excerpted from *The Book of Lilith* (Nicolas Hayes), © 1986 by Barbara Koltuv, and is used with permission of the author.

Jacqueline Lapidus. "Eden" is reprinted from *Starting Over* (Out and Out Books). © 1977 by Jacqueline Lapidus. Reprinted by permission of the author.

Jo Milgrom. "Strange Bedfellows . . . Holy Words and Demonic Images" is excerpted from "Some Second Thoughts About Adam's First Wife," which appeared in *Genesis I–III in the History of Exegesis*, ed. Gregory Allen Robbins (Edwin Mellen Press, 1988). It is used by permission of the author.

Rochelle Natt. "Lilith" is used by permission of the author.

Haviva Ner-David. "Cooking a Kid in Its Mother's Milk" is used by permission of the author.

Lesléa Newman. "Still Life with Woman and Apple" © 1994 by Lesléa Newman from *Every Woman's Dream* © 1994 Lesléa Newman (New Victoria Publishers, Norwich, VT). Reprinted by permission of the author.

Alicia Ostriker. "The Lilith Poems" appeared in Alicia Ostriker, *Feminist Revision and the Bible* (Blackwell, 1994). Reprinted by permission of the author.

Helen Papell. "Achsah at the Spring" and "Dancing-Woman" *Talking with Eve Leah Hagar Miriam* by Helen Papell (National Council of Jewish Women, New York Section, 1996). Reprinted by permission of the author.

Alix Pirani. "Cain and Abel: A Case for Family Therapy? (an excerpt). First published in *European Judaism*, this article appeared in *Body and Bible—Interpreting and Experiencing Biblical Narratives*, ed. Bjorn Krondorfer (Trinity Press International, 1992). Excerpted and published by permission of the author.

Judith Plaskow. "The Coming of Lilith" (excerpt) appeared in *Womanspirit Rising* (Harper & Row, 1973). Reprinted and excerpted by permission of the author.

Norma Fain Pratt. "What Is Your Relation to a Flower?" is used by permission of the author.

Mindy Rinkewich. "For the Lilith Archives" appeared in *The White Beyond the Forest* by Mindy Rinkewich (Cross-Cultural Communications, 1992). Reprinted by permission of the author.

Lilly Rivlin. "Lilith" was first published in *Ms.* magazine, December 1972. Reprinted by permission of the author. "Lilith Aging and Healing" © 1997 by Lilly Rivlin and "Lilith Lives" are used by permission of the author.

Lynn Saul. "To Lilith: Considerations on Women, Men, Children, and Thinking for Yourself" appeared in *Feminist Parenting*, ed. Dena Taylor (Crossing Press, 1994). Reprinted by permission of the author.

Lynne Savitt. "The Last Lilith Poem" appeared in *Lust in 28 Flavors* by Lynne Savitt (Second Coming Press, 1979). Reprinted by permission of the author.

Jane Schapiro. "Postpartum" was first published in *Black Warrior Review* (Spring/Summer 1990). Reprinted by permission of the author.

Leah Schweitzer. "In This Dream" is used by permission of the author.

Joanne Seltzer. "Lilith's Version" is used by permission of the author.

Susan Sherman. "Lilith of the Wildwood, of the Fair Places" first appeared in the *womens libeRATion* newspaper, May 22–June 1, 1971. It has been reprinted in *With Anger/With Love* (Mulch Press, 1976). © 1976 by Susan Sherman. Reprinted by permission of the author.

Layle Silbert. "Talking About Lilith" is used by permission of the author.

Frieda Singer. "Lilith's Daughters" is reprinted from *Poetpourri* (Fall 1992). Reprinted with permission of the author. "World of Our Mothers" is used by permission of the author.

Judith Skillman. "Kreis," "The Wellhouse," and "Inside Lilith" are used by permission of the author.

Julia Stein. "Lilith Grows a Garden" first appeared as "Lilith, Part II" in *Under the Ladder to Heaven* (West End Press). © 1984 by Julia Stein and is used by permission of the author.

Nikki Stiller. "Male and Female Created He Them" first appeared in *Midstream* and is reprinted by permission of the author.

Danielle Storper Perez and Henri Cohen Solal. "Lilith and Miriam" excerpted from "The Imagination of Prophecy." Edited and translated from *Les nouveaux cahiers*, no. 73 (Summer 1983). Reprinted by permission of the authors.

Savina J. Teubal. "Lilith and Hawwah" is used by permission of the author.

Henny Wenkart. Portions of "Feminist Revaluation of the Mythical Triad of Two Women and One Man: Lilith, Adam, Eve" were published in *Philosophy in the Contemporary World* 1, No. 4 (Winter 1994). It is used by permission of the author.

Ruth Whitman. "The First Woman" is used by permission of the author.

Naomi Wolf's "Introduction" is used by permission of the author.

INDEX

Aaron, 300, 301–302
Abel, 245–246, 248, 249
Abraham (Abram), 37–38, 109, 184
Achsah, 315–317, 363–366
Adam, xv, 5–9, 17–19, 28, 51, 56, 61–63, 67–68, 75, 81–83, 87–92, 95, 103, 105, 108, 115, 135–139, 148, 149, 181–184, 187–188, 192–193, 246–250, 275–276, 284, 290–291, 297–298, 299, 325, 335–336, 371, 383
Adamah,
  as mother of Adam and Lilith, 87–90, 92
  as mother of Lilith, 247, 248
  conflated with Lilith, 325
  as creation of Lilith, 333–334
Adler, Rachel, 57

Agadah, 17, 289–290
Agrat (Igrat) bat Mahalath, Queen of the Demons, 115, 224, 227, 299
Ahasueras, 284
Alphabet of Ben Sira, xvi, 6–7, 11, 18–19, 21, 26, 297, 302, 308
Amram, 300, 301–302
Amulet, 7, 9–10, 18, 106–107, 263, 290, 298, 299, 309, 310, 371
Anath, 12
Aphrodite, 27
"Ardat Lilith," 13
Aristotle, 239
Asherah, 219
Ashtoreh, 219
Astarte, 47
Athena, xviii, 213–216

Avigdor, (I.B. Singer character) 208
Azen, Margot Stein, 195, 390
Babylon, 13
Babylonia, 307, 308
Baker, Sara Eve, xviii
Belag, Andrea, 390
Benton, Suzanne, 390
Beruriah, 22, 38
Bohemian Women's Political Alliance, 390
Bramhall, John, 390
Browning, Robert, 194–195
Burton, Sue, 107, 313

Cain, 245–251, 299
Caleb, 316–317, 365
Campbell, Joseph, 6, 12, 391
Canaan, 12, 316
  fertility religion in, 56
Cantor, Aviva, 26, 192, 284, 311
Carpenter, Mary Chapin, 389
Chapman, Tracy, 389
Chasen, Lee, 390
Chelm, 225
Cohn, Cora, 390
Corelli, Marie, 391
Crow, Sheryl, 389

Daniel, Shoshona, 315
Demeter, 316
Divorce-bowls, Nippur, 308
Dodson, Betty, 392
Drattell, Deborah, 390

Eden, Garden of, xv, 18, 21, 25–26, 37, 75, 79, 98, 115, 135–139, 143, 247, 249, 276, 291, 309, 334–336
eden (Sumerian), 333

Elijah, 32–33
Elohim,
  as father of Adam and Lilith, 87–92
Esther, 17, 109–110, 284
Eve (Hava, Hawwah), xvi, xviii, 5–6, 8, 17–18, 26, 37, 43–44, 45–46, 56, 57, 63, 81–83, 105, 108, 109, 115, 135–136, 138, 182–184, 187–188, 189–195, 199, 203, 232, 246–250, 255, 275, 290, 323–324, 331, 335–336
  Christian view of, 17
  Daughters of, 37
Exodus, 300

Fishman, Louise, 390
Four Sons (Passover), 311
Franzese, Mari Anne, 390
Freud, Sigmund, 193, 308
Friday, Nancy, 392

Gabriel, 90–92
Gaia, xviii, 47, 340–341
Gemora, 208
Gemorrah (city), 38
Genesis, xvi, xviii, 5–7, 26, 55–56, 191–192, 245
Gendler, Mary, xvi
Gilgamesh, 13, 56, 309
Ginzberg, Louis, 391
Goodman, Naomi, xvi, 323
Graves, Robert, 12, 192

Hagar, 195
Hannah, 109, 195
Harris, Emmylou, 389
Hecuba, 316
Hyman, Naomi, xvii

Inanna, 47, 390, 391
Incantation bowls, 9, 56–57, 307
Indigo Girls, 389
Inquisition, 20, 375
Isaiah, xvi, 12, 30, 310, 333
Isaiah II, 30–31
Ishtar, 47, 106, 391
Isis, 391

Jacob, 109, 228, 309
Jerusalem, 225
Jochevet, 300–302
Jong, Erica, 392
Jungian Analysis, xi, 27, 323

Kabbalah, xv, xvii, 8, 18, 26, 107, 300, 309, 375
Kali, 8, 47
Katz, Nina Judith, xviii
Koltuv, Barbara, 310
Korman, Harriet, 390

Labartu, 284
Lacan, Jacques, 392, 393
Lamashtu, 284
Leah, 195
Leviton, Liz Lauren, 390
Lillim, 194
Lilin (Storm Demons), 307
"Lilith," art exhibition, 390
Lilith Fair, 389, 392
Lilith Magazine, 390
Lillu (Gilgamesh's father), 56
Loeb, Lisa, 389
Lot, 38

Madonna, xii
Mahalat, 299
McLachlan, Sarah, 389
Mendelsohn, John, 392

Medusa, 283
Meyer, Melissa, 390
Middle Ages, 8–9, 20, 21, 72, 106–107, 311, 375–376
Midrash, xv, xvi, 17, 20, 55, 56, 106, 290, 299, 301, 310, 316
  Contemporary Midrash, xvi, xvii, xix, 310, 317, 323–324, 392
Milstein, Rebecca, 105–106
Miriam, 26, 27, 28–30, 32, 33–34, 295, 300–303, 311, 316
Miriam's Well, 302, 316–317, 365
Mitsvot, 302
Moses, 26, 27, 28–30, 33, 300
Ms Magazine, xvii, 391, 392

Naamah (Naama), 11, 299, 325
Naomi, 195
Nile, 301
Niobe, 316
Nippur (Babylonia), 57, 307
Noah, 309, 353

Osborne, Joan, 389
Oshun, 47
Ostriker, Alicia, xvi, xvii
Othniel, 316

Papell, Helen, xviii, 315–317
Patai, Raphael, 10, 12, 26, 309–310, 314, 391
Penninah, 195
Pirani, Alix, xviii
Plaskow, Judith, xvi, 195, 323
Pratt, Norma Fain, xviii
Puah, 301

Rabbinate, 95-98
Rabbinical tradition, 7
Rabbis, xv, 6, 182n
Rachel, 109, 195, 225
Raphael, 90-92
Red Sea, xv, 5, 7, 21, 23, 26-30, 32, 34, 90-91, 143, 145-154, 207, 223-224, 226, 309, 311, 336, 391
  in Babylonian cosmogony, 27
Rivlin, Lilly, xiii, xv, xvii
Rodham, Hillary (Clinton), xii
Rossetti, Dante Gabriel, 391
Ruth, xvi, 195

Sabbath, 312
Samael, 9, 18, 22, 309
Samuel, 109
Sarah (Sarai), xvi, 37-38, 109, 195
Saul, Lynn, 315
Savitt, Lynne, xviii
Schapiro, Jane, xviii, 314
Schecter, David, 195, 390
Scholem, Gershom, 26
Schweitzer, Leah, xviii
Seboulisa, 47
Semangelaf, 95, 224, 228, 263
Senoi (Sanvi), 95, 224, 228, 263
Sensoi (Sansanvi), 95, 224, 228, 263
Serpentine
  (composer-performer), 390
Seth, 194, 249, 250
Shakespeare, William, 107
Shaw, Bernard, 195
Sheba, Queen of, 11, 115
Shekinah, 47, 219, 250, 309, 312-313, 324-325
  conflated with Lilith, 251, 314
  as Matronit, 312
Sherman, Susan, xvii
Shifra, 301
Silbert, Layle, xviii
Singer, I.B., 207-208
Singer-Kreitman, Hinde-Esther, xviii, 207-208
Snyder, Joan, 390
Sodom, 38
Solomon, 11, 309
Stanton, Elizabeth Cady, 193
Starr, Kinnie, 389
Stein, Julia, 315
Sumeria, 13, 56, 308

Talmud, xv, 11, 38, 56, 308, 310, 348
Tanach, 208
Tannen, Deborah, 106
Tiamet, 27, 30
Teubal, Savina, xvi, xviii
Thelma and Louise (film), xii
Torah, 302
  study of 300
Tree of Knowledge, 37, 88, 135, 136, 335-336
Tree of Life, 335, 336

Uriel, 90-92
Uroboros, 143, 154

Vashti, xvi, 109-110
Virgin Mary, 8, 34, 47
  Black Virgin, 391

Whitman, Ruth, xviii
Wittig, Monique, 325
Wolf, Naomi, 392

Yemaya (Yemanja), 27, 47
Yentl (I.B. Singer character), 208

Zeresh (Haman's wife), 110
Zipporah, 34
Zohar, 9, 18, 26, 28, 32, 297, 298, 299, 309, 311, 314

About the Editors

Enid Dame is a poet, writer, and lecturer at the New Jersey Institute of Technology. She received her doctorate in English literature from Rutgers University. Her books of poems include *Anything You Don't See*, *Confessions*, and the midrashic *Lilith and Her Demons*. Her poems, fiction, and essays have appeared in many publications, including *Tikkun*, *Wise Words*, *Her Face in the Mirror*, *The Tribe of Dina*, *Phoebe: An Interdisciplinary Feminist Journal*, *Sarah's Daughters Sing*, and *Modern Poems on the Bible*. She has received a New York State Creative Artist in Public Service Grant for poetry and a Puffin Foundation grant for a novel-in-progress. She lives in Brooklyn and High Falls, New York, with her husband, the poet Donald Lev, with whom she co-edits the literary tabloid *Home Planet News*.

Lilly Rivlin, a seventh-generation Jerusalemite, is a writer and filmmaker specializing in Jewish and international subjects. She is a veteran journalist whose work has appeared in national publications, which include *Newsweek*, *Ms.*, *The Washington Post*, and *US* magazine, as well as Jewish periodicals. She was principal researcher on *O Jerusalem*, a book by Larry Collins and Dominique Lapierre. Her film credits include *The Tribe* and *Miriam's Daughters Now*. Ms. Rivlin, one of the founders of the Feminist Seder, creates rituals and *midrash*, and gives workshops on biblical texts from a woman's point of view. She lives in New York City.

Henny Wenkart is the editor of the *Jewish Women's Literary Annual*. She holds a Ph.D in Philosophy from Harvard and an M.S. in Journalism from Columbia. Among her other books are the poetry anthology *Sarah's Daughters Sing*, the translation of Pauline Wengeroff's *Memoirs of a Grandmother*, and six children's books, including *Get Off the Desk!* and *The Big Puppet Mix-Up*. She is a member of the Editorial Board of the Scholarly Edition of the works of George Santayana, and the Board of Harvard-Radcliffe Hillel, among others. Her poems and philosophical articles have appeared in many anthologies and literary journals. She is married and lives in New York City and Cambridge, Massachusetts. She and her husband have three children and a number of grandchildren.